"In a world full of noise, *Powerful Self-Talk from the Psalms* helps you tune your inner voice to truth. A wise and winsome companion for anyone longing to hear—and speak—God's words over their life."

—**Les Parrott, PhD**, #1 *New York Times*
bestselling author of *Love Like That*

"I love this book for its practicality, its application to my heart, and its recognition that we must talk to ourselves in a better way. We must learn from David how to talk to ourselves about our need to stay focused on the Lord. When I began reading *Powerful Self-Talk from the Psalms*, I found myself reading it all in one sitting because one chapter made me anticipate and thirst for the next. Now I shall go through it more thoughtfully each day, letting each chapter sink into my soul.

Let me give you a suggestion: Get several copies of this book and give it as a gift to those who are spiritually weary, those who are seeking help on how to focus on the Lord, and those who are not yet Christians but are open to the idea of self-talk and prayer. Because of its relevance to our hearts, this is a book for us all."

—**Erwin W. Lutzer**, pastor emeritus, Moody Church Chicago

"My friend Jon Gauger has given us a great guide to transitioning from the self-talk that often compounds our sense of distress to the God-talk that brings courage, confidence, and peace amid the challenges of life! The Psalms have always been my go-to when I needed a word from God in the face of difficulty. Yet sometimes I wonder where to go given the wide expanse of the book. Thankfully, Jon has offered us a guide, with relevant insights, into the wisdom of the Psalms. *Powerful Self-Talk from the Psalms* provides us with a way to talk ourselves into His talk. Thanks, Jon. We needed this!"

—**Joe Stowell**, global ambassador and special assistant
to the president at Moody Bible Institute

"Too often that voice in your head, the one that sounds like you, is condemning and belittling. Jon Gauger wants us to know that self-talk from the Psalms is how we replace condemnation with comfort, loathing with loving, and pain with peace. Join him on the journey of discovering how to replace that troublesome self-talk with God's perfect voice."

—**Janet Parshall**, nationally syndicated host/author

"When it comes to talking to myself, I can't stop it—and neither can you! But, as Jon teaches, we can change it. Jon does a remarkable job of drawing out Psalms we can use as tools to fix our broken self-talk. One I really loved was 'sleep talk.' As an almost Olympic-level insomniac, I was so blessed by Jon's teaching on Psalm 4. It has been incredibly helpful, and that's just one example of the many practical truths you'll find in this book. So put your destructive self-talk on notice! It's about to be out of your thoughts, vocabulary, and life for good! And I mean...for good."

—**Jennifer Rothschild**, author of 20 books and Bible studies, including *Lessons I Learned in the Dark* and *Heaven: When Faith Becomes Sight*

"In *Powerful Self-Talk from the Psalms*, Jon Gauger, my good friend and radio cohost, shares bite-sized bits of wisdom gleaned from the book of Psalms to help someone respond biblically to life's problems and pressures. This is a book you need to read slowly and carefully—perhaps a chapter a day—to give yourself time to put each truth into practice. (Jon provides very practical steps for doing so at the end of each chapter.) Follow his wise advice, and you'll start to see your thoughts and actions parallel those of King David, who was a man after God's own heart!"

—**Dr. Charles Dyer**, Professor-at-Large of Bible and host of *The Land and the Book* radio program, Moody Bible Institute

"I started recommending Jon Gauger's new book to my family and friends after reading just two chapters. The reason it made such an impact on me is because I had the same struggle Jon did with negative self-talk. But Jon dove headfirst into the Scriptures and learned valuable lessons from King David himself. Who doesn't battle with a parade of negative thoughts that often run through our mind? The enemy launches these mind-missiles nonstop at us, and they can dominate our thoughts if we don't learn how to overcome them. *Powerful Self-Talk from the Psalms* is a life-preserver for your mind and soul. I highly recommend it!"

—**Tom Doyle,** author of *Dreams and Visions: Is Jesus Awakening the Muslim World?* and CEO and cofounder of Uncharted Ministries

"What might happen at the soul level if you were to change the negative dialog you have with your heart? Jon Gauger has found transforming truth straight from the ancient poetry of the Bible. Change the script, and your life will change for the better."

—**Chris Fabry,** author and host of *Chris Fabry Live* on Moody Radio

"You will find *Powerful Self-Talk from the Psalms* to be healing for the heart and salve for the soul. Jon Gauger writes fluidly—often humorously—and honestly about real issues we would rather avoid, such as turning from evil or getting back to kneeling when we pray. Wherever you are as a Christian, *Powerful Self-Talk from the Psalms* will stimulate your spiritual journey."

—**Dr. Woodrow Kroll**, president and senior Bible teacher (retired), Back to the Bible International

"Some books are meant to be read; this book is meant to be lived. We all engage in self-talk, so why not fill it with the liberating truth of God's Word? Jon brilliantly captures this in *Powerful Self-Talk from the Psalms*. Whether overcoming condemnation or embracing humility under God's mighty hand, this book will realign your words and life with God's powerful truth. I've witnessed how Jon's passion for the Bible has transformed him, and I know it can do the same for you. Embrace this journey, and watch your own life be transformed!"

—**Karl Clauson,** host of nationally syndicated *Karl and Crew* on Moody radio affiliates, pastor, and author

"Reading Jon Gauger is never a slog. It's a delight to breeze through his engaging insights. I nod my head, pause at breakthrough moments, and marvel at how he somehow knows exactly what I'm thinking. Maybe it's because, as a longtime Moody Radio listener, I hear Jon's voice as I read. Which works well with this book, because the Psalms are meant to be spoken, sung, and shared aloud. So, thanks, Jon. The Psalms are suddenly a fresh source of joy and encouragement for me. And, honestly, your voice in my head is not as painful as it sounds."

—**Jay Payleitner,** national speaker and bestselling author of *52 Things Kids Need from a Dad*, *A Grand Way to Live*, and *What If God Wrote Your Bucket List?*

"It's time to think about what you are thinking about! Instead of worrying about the news or comparing yourself to others on social media, you can choose to think about what the Bible says about your life. Your perspective will change for the better as you examine the Psalms more closely through this book!"

—**Arlene Pellicane,** author of *Parents Rising* and host of the *Happy Home* podcast

"The Psalms have ministered to me for more than 40 years. While some may not love poetry, a careful, lingering study of the Psalms is a life-changing discipline. In *Powerful Self-Talk from the Psalms*, Jon guides you to dwell in the structure, meaning, and application of these rich song-hymns laden with emotion, theology, and history. I am grateful Jon has worked diligently to help us get our nose in the Book."

—**Michael Easley,** pastor, former president Moody Bible Institute

"If we want to know the will of God, it is found in the Word of God. It didn't take long for me to meet myself in Jon's book. The Psalms are the perfect balm needed to penetrate the pitfalls and problems in life. *Powerful Self-Talk from the Psalms* is so personal it feels as though it was written just for me."

—**Tammy Whitehurst,** motivational speaker and writer

"Delightful, practical, personal, and a good way to enjoying the Psalms! Jon suggests a healthy approach to self-image and controlling our thoughts. In keeping with biblical emphasis, he helps us to govern our thought life. The illustrations he uses are instructive in encouraging us to keep our thoughts aligned with the truth of the Bible throughout the day."

—**Dr. C. Fred Dickason**, professor emeritus of theology, Moody Bible Institute

"Jon Gauger's *Powerful Self-Talk from the Psalms* is touching and real. Between his blend of personal experiences and biblical and practical examples, I had a hard time putting it down! Reading Jon's book felt like a close friend guiding me through real-life problems and their biblical solutions."

—**Joslynn Jaeger,** YA novelist

"*Powerful Self-Talk from the Psalms* previews the path I have seen Jon and his precious wife walk along the way. Through the years, his biblical insights and encouragement have been truly refreshing to me as our friendship has grown. This resource contains crucial life lessons that will prove to be both enjoyable and challenging."

—**David C. Gibbs**, Jr., attorney-at-law

POWERFUL SELF-TALK from the PSALMS

JON GAUGER

HARVEST HOUSE PUBLISHERS
EUGENE, OREGON

Italics in Scripture verses indicate emphasis by the author.

Published in association with the literary agency of the Steve Laube Agency, LLC, 24 W. Camelback Rd. A-635, Phoenix, Arizona 85013.

Cover design and images custom created by Faceout Studio

Interior design by KUHN Design Group

For bulk, special sales, or ministry purchases, please call 1-800-547-8979.
Email: CustomerService@hhpbooks.com

Powerful Self-Talk from the Psalms

Published by Harvest House Publishers
Eugene, Oregon 97408
www.harvesthousepublishers.com

ISBN 978-0-7369-9183-4 (pbk)
ISBN 978-0-7369-9184-1 (eBook)

Library of Congress Control Number: 2025936296

Printed in the United States of America

25 26 27 28 29 30 31 32 33 / VP / 10 9 8 7 6 5 4 3 2 1

To our children and their godly spouses:

Lynnette and her husband, Josh

Tim and his wife, Bethany

• • •

Diana and I are grateful for you, proud of you, and love you beyond words.

Keep following after Christ—you and your children.

Earth is fading. Heaven approaches. Keep the faith!

ACKNOWLEDGMENTS

A simple thank-you is too small for the investment of my wife, Diana, who tweaked the first draft of every chapter—and kindly, graciously, and selflessly lived with me through the whole process. You are amazing. (I think you're "sometheen elff!").

I am also indebted to:

- Dr. Michael Easley, whose excellent teaching planted a love for the Psalms deep in my soul.
- Godly mentors like Dr. Charlie Dyer, Dr. Bob Moeller, Pastor Jim Lennon, Russ Caforio, and Dr. Fred Dickason.
- Kathy Dyer, a proofreader *par excellence*, who kept my writing on the straight and narrow grammar path.

How grateful I am for friends who encourage me to write. Among them are Jerry Jenkins, Jay Payleitner, Bill Davis, Dan Anderson, Lee Rugen, Chris Segard, Chris Fabry, Jon Hemmer, Vyto Miknaitis, Steve Kluth—and my dad, David. Also, Colin and Geri Brewer and our mutual friend, J.A.

Thanks to Dan Balow—agent of astonishing efficiency—and thanks to the team at the Steve Laube Agency.

Aaron Johnson has kindly, creatively, and selflessly maintained my website from day one, and I am surely in his debt.

It's an honor to team up with Harvest House Publishers again, and I will always be indebted to Kim Moore, who first opened the door for me here. Her careful and kind expertise and oversight have guided this project with the utmost class and professionalism.

CONTENTS

FOREWORD

JERRY JENKINS

Could it be a coincidence that for several days I'd been reminded of two of my favorite verses from the Bible before I was privileged to write a foreword to Jon Gauger's latest book?

I think not.

For decades I've believed that Psalm 91:1-2 (NKJV) comprise some of the most beautiful sentences ever translated into English.

> He who dwells in the secret place of the Most High
> Shall abide under the shadow of the Almighty.
> I will say of the LORD, "He is my refuge and my fortress;
> My God, in Him I will trust."

And yes, I often use those sentiments as self-talk. What could be more thrilling, more self-assuring, more comforting than dwelling in the secret place of the Most High, abiding under the shadow of the Almighty, and being able to say of the Lord that He is my refuge and my fortress?

Imagine my delight, then, in discovering that longtime friend Jon Gauger has made *Powerful Self-Talk from the Psalms* his most recent subject. I love the tack he takes that clarifies his view of himself—not a theologian, not a scholar (but I can tell you he's a pretty smart guy), not even a master of the very effort he espouses here. Rather, he's a regular guy, a fellow struggler in the self-talk world.

But he's learned a lot—much of it the hard way. And that's what we get here. Lots of everyday, real-people stories, examples of folks we can identify with and learn from. Jon has never backed away from hard truth, and neither has he ever apologized for wanting to be more like Christ. Helping us get there too is his clear aim here.

Enjoy the journey. I sure have.

Jerry B. Jenkins
Novelist and biographer

INTRODUCTION

We talk to ourselves.

All day, every day. And a lot of those messages are self-condemning. We say things like:

- Why haven't you made more progress overcoming that habit?
- How could you think this ministry is something you could actually do?
- God might answer this colossal need for others—but don't expect it to happen for you.
- You're not smart enough, good-looking enough, or talented enough.
- What kind of a Bible study leader would say something that hurtful?
- Obviously, you're not praying right or praying enough, or this problem would go away.
- Face it. You'll always struggle with this issue.

Do any of those statements sound familiar? Of course! But how can we hope for damage control when *we* are the ones doing the damage? We can't shut off our minds. Nor can we shut down the reality that we talk to ourselves anymore than we can keep our eyes from blinking, our lungs from breathing, or our heart from beating.

What we need is a model for better self-talk. That's exactly what David offers us. *Powerful Self-Talk from the Psalms* is a practical guide for learning biblical self-talk. I know it works (because I need it the most), and I've experienced what can happen when I talk like David.

Let me tell you a quick story. On Monday I flew from Chicago to Colorado Springs to record an important interview. Naturally, I took along my trusty iPad. During the nearly three-hour flight, I did some freelance writing, worked on a Sunday school lesson, and wrote a blog—all on my beloved device.

Upon landing, I grabbed my gear, exited the plane, and plopped my backpack on a chair to get reorganized. Only upon arriving at the interview location a couple of hours later did I realize what I'd left behind at the airport gate. You've already guessed it—my iPad.

My response? I did what ordinary people do at moments like this: I beat myself up for stupid irresponsibility. How could I have been so careless, so foolish? A net of anxiety—laced with thorny bramble—fell all over my soul, and I was bleeding emotionally.

For me, the iPad is much more than a tablet to surf the web, check email, or play a game. I practically live on it. It's my laptop. I've written entire books on it. And it contained articles, blogs, sermons, and book chapters (still unfinished) that were about to be lost forever. The thought of losing all that investment made me nauseous.

The Grand-Champion Worrywart in me started to curl up in a ball and moan. Just 24 hours previously—Sunday morning—I'd preached a sermon based on Psalm 25:15. It says this: "My eyes are continually toward the LORD, for He will rescue my feet from the net."

A light flashed in my soul, and I realized this was a moment when I needed to talk like David. Know what I did? I prayed with a friend, quoting that verse. Next, we called the airport, filled out an online form, and waited.

All afternoon, I fought off repeated blasts of anxiety with the same indestructible weapon—the Word of God. Over and over, I said, "My eyes are continually toward the Lord, for He will rescue my feet from the net." While I still felt a measure of concern (and guilt), this verse brought sanity and structure to a thought life under siege.

At dinner that evening, my phone rang. Again, you've already guessed who was on the line—the airport. Unthinkably, some honest soul had turned in my iPad, and I could pick it up at the airline baggage counter immediately. I wasted no time in reclaiming it.

Now, I'm not suggesting that God will always step in and bail us out when we do foolish things. but I am saying His Word can enable us to walk through trouble in a God-honoring way without bashing ourselves in the process. Even if God had chosen not to reunite me with that iPad, I would be able to look back at the day and know that instead of being immobilized by a net of anxiety, I had chosen to turn my eyes toward the Lord continually.

I'm sure you could tell me a few stories from your journey. No doubt you've heard of the blame game, but many of us play the *shame game*. We've become unintentional champions at bashing our souls. But aren't you tired of trashing yourself? Don't you long for a better way to speak to your soul? Then learn powerful self-talk from the book of Psalms.

David had real problems.

We have real problems.

The difference is David learned to speak to himself in ways that led to better thinking, better choices, and better living. So stop talking like you. Talk instead like David.

You'll be amazed at how easy and natural it becomes to borrow his thoughts, attitudes, and very words to begin making an immediate difference in your life.

This is not a lightweight book. It's a tool kit for fixing what must not remain broken. When it comes to self-talk, we can't stop it. But we *can* fix it. And that's what this book is all about.

To be clear, this is not another commentary on the book of Psalms. Nor is it primarily a book of theology. These chapters will connect you with only a handful of the 150 psalms that make up the complete collection in the Bible. My aim was to sift through *some* of David's self-talk and apply it to modern life—yours and mine.

For me, this is much more than a book. It's become a way of life. I have committed myself for the long term to continue down this road of learning to talk like David. Speaking Scripture to my own doubts and negative thoughts is the only way I've found to correct my self-talk. I don't see this as merely helpful or important. I think this idea is urgent.

My goal for you? I want you to grab hold of these verses and prove to yourself that God's Word has the power to calm your fears, build your hope, and grow your faith. I want you to walk away from this experience utterly amazed at the very personal impact of God's Word.

This book will equip you with tools to shape biblical self-talk. And that impact will begin for you starting with the very first chapter. You cannot quote Scripture without benefiting from Scripture.

To find your self-talk in the psalms is to talk biblically. To talk biblically is to honor God. To honor God is to be blessed by God—in this life and the life to come.

Enough of our negative self-talk. Let's replace it—*all* of it—with powerful self-talk from the psalms. Because it's time to rethink your "think" and reclaim your brain.

1

SLEEP SAFE, LIVE SAFE

In peace I will both lie down and sleep,
for You alone, Lord, have me dwell in safety.

PSALM 4:8

Count on it. Anyone who claims they sleep like a baby definitely does not have one. Our firstborn was almost an only child because she virtually refused to sleep. Now, with four children of her own, she remains an incredibly light sleeper.

But, boy, do we need our sleep! Without it, we become like tall two-year-olds, right? If only sleep came (and stayed) easily.

The National Heart, Lung, and Blood Institute estimates that between 50 and 70 million Americans have ongoing sleep disorders.[1]

In America, drowsy driving causes more than 6,000 fatal car crashes annually. Who knew that insufficient sleep has an estimated economic impact of more than $411 billion annually in the United States?[2]

The problem is so widespread that 56 percent of adults have consumed at least one sleep aid in the past month.[3]

And it's hardly a once-in-a-while problem. According to the Centers for Disease Control, 8 percent of adults say they took medication to help them sleep at least four times in the past week.[4]

Maybe you feel like the guy who reluctantly woke up, and the first mumbled words out of his mouth were, "I already want to take a nap." But odds are, your biggest challenge is not getting up—it's getting to sleep.

Of course, there are as many reasons for sleepless nights as there are pills to make us drowsy:

- Too much caffeine...not enough exercise.
- Too much screen time...not enough quiet time.
- We eat too often...we eat too much...we eat too late.

But I'm not here to judge you, lecture you, or even educate you. I'm here to encourage you.

If any of the usual sleep-depriving suspects are on your list, you probably already know what to do. But what about the rest of us—the most of us—who have already tried to root out the usual suspects? What if we have cut back on the caffeine, turned down the noise, and unplugged from our screens after supper, but we still struggle with sleep?

Medical issues are undoubtedly real, and there's no reason not to go to a doctor to rule these out. But let's say you've done that and sleep is still elusive. Is it possible there's a critical component we lack? What is the one vital quality we absolutely must have for quality sleep?

That one essential quality is peace. King David put his finger on it in a fascinating self-talk secret we find in Psalm 4:8. David says, "In peace I will both lie down and sleep, for You alone, Lord, have me dwell in safety."

Because this sleep problem of ours is so huge, and because so much is packed into this one verse, what do you say we take an unhurried stroll through what I like to call David's "Sanctified Sleep Study." In this extraordinary verse, David lets us in on his nighttime ritual before he pillows his head. It's not just self-talk—it's sleep talk.

Check out his first phrase, "In peace." It's the backbone on which the rest of the verse hangs. We're kidding ourselves if we think we're going to enjoy quality sleep without real peace in our heart. So where do we get it? Jesus.

Jesus said the peace He offers is "not as the world gives" (John 14:27). In other words, it's not fake. Every year, the cash amount of counterfeit goods sold around the globe is between $1.7 trillion and $4.5 trillion, making knockoff products the world's tenth-largest economy.[5]

There's something exquisite about the brand of peace the Prince of Peace offers. This is no knockoff.

And then Jesus adds, "Do not let your hearts be troubled, nor fearful." Bear in mind, this peace was in effect even as Jesus prepared Himself to be whipped, beaten, and crucified. Whatever it is you're going through, it's not as bad as that. You can have peace right in the middle of your unresolved chapter.

Next, David says, "In peace, I will both lie down and sleep." Don't you love the fact that he separates the two? It's so easy to lie down—and sometimes so hard to sleep! But David says the peace given by the Prince of Peace is sufficiently rest inducing for both. In other words, His peace is enough. Enough for you. Enough to bring sleep to your sleepless nights.

As we continue with David's sleep study, note the following phrase, "For You alone, Lord, have me dwell in safety." Note that we don't have occasional visits with safety. We *live* there. In Christ, and because of Christ, we "dwell in safety." Safety is our street address.

Have you ever noticed that your address says a lot about you? Right or wrong, people make assumptions about you based on where you live. With Jesus, you're on the safe side of the tracks. You live in a house called *Peace* on a street called *Peace* in a town called *Peace* ruled by the *Prince of Peace*.

One catch, though. David reminds himself (and us) that all this good stuff comes from one Source, one Person—the Lord. He says, "For You alone, LORD…"

HOW TO MAKE THIS SELF-TALK YOURS

We're not going to find this peace in conversations with our friends and loved ones. We're not going to find this peace in the latest Christian conference or a bestselling devotional. No, the verse spells it out: "For You alone, LORD, have me dwell in safety."

In Christ—and only in Christ—you have all the peace you need for all the sleep you need. Doesn't that sound awesome? Say it to yourself out loud right now: "In peace I will both lie down and sleep, for You alone, LORD, have me dwell in safety."

Next time sleep refuses to come, sing this lullaby. Just remember that it's more than a song. It's the essence of sleep.

Why not trade in your old negative self-talk for something biblical? Why not enjoy the rest God has promised? It's time to start sleeping like a baby.

• • •

SAY IT

"In peace I will both lie down and sleep,
for You alone, Lord, have me dwell in safety."

PSALM 4:8

PRAY IT

Prince of Peace—

I praise You that in You I am safe—and can sleep in complete confidence. I am…

- safe in my unsolved problems
- safe in my imperfect family
- safe in my health issues
- safe in my job

Most of all, I am safe in my eternal destiny because of what Jesus accomplished on the cross in paying for every wrongdoing I've done in the past and will do in the future

Thank You that, as Jesus promised, no one can take me out of the Father's hand.

Thank You that because of Christ, I can lie down and sleep safely.

I praise You and thank You, my Prince of Peace.

Amen.

2

AT YOUR RIGHT HAND

I have set the Lord *continually before me;*
because He is at my right hand, I will not be shaken.

PSALM 16:8

When was the last time you were not just sick, but *really* sick? Sick, as in you didn't get out of bed for a couple of days. Or maybe you ended up in the ER.

One frustrated wife frequently complained of not feeling well but thought her husband rarely noticed or cared. So she secretly paid a monument company to make her headstone in advance. It featured her name, her date of birth, and this statement: "I told you I was sick!"

When I visit people in the hospital, I find a similarity to what they keep on the tray table next to their bed: not much. Whether recovering at home or in a hospital, a sick person carefully considers what they keep within arm's reach: water, medication, phone, and, of course, a TV remote. You might also have a book or iPad if your sickness is not debilitating.

The point is, when you know you're feeling trashed, the inventory of things you keep at hand is relatively small. And every chosen item is essential to you.

But what about when you're down, spiritually—when the sickness is in your *soul*? What do you keep at hand then?

I don't know about you, but I confess to being easily shaken up. A critical email, a negative text, tension at work—it doesn't take much, and I'm all shaken up. At times like these, many of us revert to unhelpful self-talk. We say, "Yeah, I'm easily upset by people and problems that oppose me, but that's just who I am."

Maybe. But that isn't who you *have* to be.

David addresses this soul sickness when he invites us to better self-talk in Psalm 16:8. His personal testimony—his coping strategy—is this: "I have set the Lord continually before me; because He is at my right hand, I will not be shaken."

There's lots to ponder here. As we begin, let's bear in mind the phrase "at my right hand." In Bible times, this expression spoke of favor and importance. Note that Scripture often speaks of Jesus being at the right hand of God—again, the highest place of honor and significance (Mark 16:19; Romans 8:34; Ephesians 1:20; Colossians 3:1; Hebrews 8:1; and many more). Does your Outlook calendar and your daily routine place Christ at the highest place of honor and significance? Here are four keys that will help unlock a more biblical self-talk.

KEY #1—YOU CHOOSE TO SET HIM BEFORE YOU

Setting the Lord before you doesn't happen by default or accident. It's a choice. David said, "I have set," not "the *Lord* came to set."

No competent bricklayer just "happened" to build a straight wall. And no one ever "happened" to become a piano virtuoso the day of their first lesson. And I defy you to name a single athlete who just "happened" to win a medal at the Olympics. These things begin with a decision. We set our mind and heart on a goal—and then we follow through.

KEY #2—YOU MAKE A DAILY DECISION

Setting the Lord before you is not a one-time thing. It's a daily, *moment-by-moment* action. Note the word "continually."

An awful lot of us pay a whole lot of money for subscription plans: internet, phone, TV, cloud storage, and so on. We set up autopay with our bills, autofill with our prescriptions, and even auto-order pet supplies. But there's no "auto plan" for setting the Lord continually before you. It's something you do every day.

Like many folks, I try to get in 10,000 steps daily (my best year peaked at a daily average of 13,529). But early on, I noticed that getting in those steps demands continual commitment. Every. Single. Day.

If you want your yearly average to be high, your daily average must be high. So you are—continually—focused on your steps. Same thing with setting the Lord before you. It's a continual thing (as in all throughout your day).

KEY #3—YOU INVITE HIS PRESENCE TO BE WITH YOU

Setting the Lord before you continually invites the Lord's continual presence to be in your life. To be clear, other verses, like Hebrews 13:5, remind us that, as believers, we have the Lord with us and in us. Still, there's everything to be said for a continual choice to set the Lord before us consciously. It creates a sense of God-awareness we might otherwise lack.

David says, "Because He is at my right hand, I will not be shaken." I'm so glad David doesn't say, "I'm pretty sure God will show up to protect me when I need Him most." He reminds himself that God is—already (right now and today and tomorrow)—"at my right hand."

Tim Tebow reminds us, "When our self-worth crumbles, when we're not feeling confident, when insecurities overwhelm us, we have to remember whose we are. It's pretty amazing how our identity lays the groundwork for everything."[1]

KEY #4—YOU SET THE LORD AT YOUR RIGHT HAND

Failing to set the Lord at your right hand has enormous negative consequences. For starters, you walk in your flesh rather than by the Spirit, which adds up to trouble really fast.

I once phoned a donor to say thanks for his gift. He contacted us early in the morning during our fundraiser, and we typically call these folks back immediately to thank them. However, the man greeted me with not one but two swear words—until I mentioned I was from his Christian radio station. Faster than Han Solo took the Millennium Falcon to light speed, this guy blasted me with charm and warmth, his every word drenched in Christianese.

Now, maybe that guy was just having a bad day, but I'm guessing he could not say like David, "I have set the LORD continually before me." What about you?

One last thought. Notice that nothing is offered to folks who set the Lord before them once in a while or only on Sundays. Which is why we need David's self-talk continually.

HOW TO MAKE THIS SELF-TALK YOURS

When is the right time to do this? Right now. We don't wait for the disturbing email about company layoffs. We don't wait for the devastating phone call from the doctor. We don't wait for the bad times to come. We set the Lord before us continually, starting now.

Here's a three-step application I recommend. First, memorize this verse. It's not long, but it is power packed. When you memorize it, you can quickly call it to mind.

Second, consider committing every morning to God with this verse. Start each day well.

Third, invite the Lord to help you call this verse to mind when stress comes knocking. I encourage you to say Psalm 16:8 out loud the very next instant you feel tense. I promise you, that trouble will loosen its grip even as you sense God tightening *His* grip on you.

This habit, this lifestyle, is the self-talk we need.

• • •

SAY IT

"I have set the Lord continually before me; because He is at my right hand, I will not be shaken."

PSALM 16:8

PRAY IT

O Lord—

You know my weary, wimpy heart.

You know how easily I am unsettled, how quickly I succumb to rumblings without and rumblings within.

But I long to live at a different level—the unshaken level.

Help me adopt David's self-talk as my own.

Then, my soul will no longer be sick.

Then, I will no longer be shaken.

Let every choice I make today reflect my desire to set the Lord before me continually.

Amen.

3

HEART'S INTENT

My intent is that my mouth will not offend.

PSALM 17:3

Intentions matter. They are the forces that guide our choices and our actions.

Consider the world's deadliest nuclear weapon—Russia's Tsar Bomba. During a test explosion, it created a mushroom cloud 37 miles tall. Buildings a hundred miles away from the blast site were damaged or destroyed—and the flash from the detonation was visible from 620 miles away. Note—none of that happened by accident. The world's most potent human-made explosion was created with intention.[1]

But consider this: Our mouths can be weapons of mass destruction too. Yours and mine. This is far from hyperbole. Your mouth is capable of creating death, devastation, grief, and isolation.

Before anyone pushes the button to launch a nuclear bomb, there are protocols, launch codes, and security checks. Oddly, the devastation our mouths create is done with little or no forethought at all. That's precisely why we must be concerned about our intentions.

Which leads me to a strategic question. Do you begin the day with the thought, *I intend to keep my mouth under control today*?

One guy quipped, "I tried keeping my mouth shut once. Worst two minutes of my life." I'm guessing most of us can relate to that frustration.

Of the many times you have hurt someone with your words, how many of those incidents were deliberate on your part? How many friendship-fracturing, confidence-killing, sister-slashing, brother-bruising verbal blasts were premediated? Did you honestly set out to injure a loved one with your speech?

My guess is if you know and love Jesus, you don't deliberately trash others with your words. Yet it happens. Which means we're guilty.

Imagine pulling out a revolver or rifle and just blasting away while whirling around in a circle, eyes closed. Not just ridiculous, this could be deadly! Just today, you might already have said something you now regret. Or maybe, at this very moment, you are simmering, determined to put someone in their place with a killer conversation that's been smoldering for hours or days.

Perhaps you feel like the guy who conceded, "My mouth has a mind of its own, but my brain has a restraining order."

May I be transparent with you? I regret—no, let me rephrase that—I really, really, *really* regret the conversations I've initiated that gashed the soul of another.

As bad as all that is, if we're not careful, we can create even worse damage by believing our broken self-talk. Jesus warns in Luke 6:45, "His mouth speaks from that which fills his heart."

We make our first mistake by surrendering control over our speech. We surrender to our feelings and our circumstances. But those of us with broken self-talk often follow it up with something equally unhelpful.

Guilty—even pained—because of our poor mouth management, many of us indulge in twisted self-talk like this, "Sure, I have trouble shooting off my mouth, but that's just how I am." What we're (dishonestly) saying is, "It's not really on me. Blame it on my DNA. Or my dysfunctional family history. Or my hideous job. Or my dog."

In the eyes of God, who sees and hears all our words, we can't simply divest ourselves from the responsibility we wish we could shuck.

Biblically speaking, mouth control is the ultimate self-control. James 3:2 says, "We all stumble in many ways. If anyone does not stumble in what he says, he is a perfect man, able to rein in the whole body as well."

Here's the blunt truth: You sound better with your mouth shut. Me too. And that's never truer than when our pulse is jacked and our nostrils flare in anger. "Great," you say. "Then what *should* I be telling myself when I feel like exploding?"

In Psalm 17:3, David said, "My intent is that my mouth will not offend." He is not saying what many of us say (without actually saying it): "Gee, I don't mean to be offensive if I am." That's neither an apology nor an action plan.

What's yours—your action plan, I mean? Maybe you have heard about the guy who claimed, "I have a black belt in keeping my mouth shut. It's called duct tape." I suppose that's one strategy. But I promise you, there's not enough duct tape in the world to restrain your mouth when the fangs of a foe inject enough venom into your pride.

Back to the action plan of David's—that better self-talk. He said, "My intent is that my mouth will not offend." He's not claiming to be perfect. He is essentially saying, "I need a battle plan *before* I get near the battle." He has a clear intention.

David's battle plan includes a bold commitment: "I have a goal, a standard for my speech. I know I'm fallible, and sinful speech comes easily, naturally. Therefore, my intent is that my mouth will not offend." David is saying, "*This* is the goal. *This* is my standard of conduct."

I've seen this verse thrive in my life. I know it works. Just as I know how miserably I fail when I don't intend to intend:

- A juicy bit of gossip is being shared, and I have something I'm tempted to add...

- A friend is being critical of someone, and I'm tempted to chime in…
- I'm angry and feel like blasting the fury of my wrath…

At that moment, we need David's self-talk: "My intent is that my mouth will not offend." Just ask the marvelous Marvin Muggins. You say you've never heard of him? Okay, so he's a character in my imagination, but you might just relate to him more than you know:

Marvelous Marvin Muggins had a million good intentions.
He collected them like coins or stamps or toys.
He just pretended he intended, but he followed through on none.
So he lost out on at least a million joys.

HOW TO MAKE THIS SELF-TALK YOURS

Don't be like Marvin. Instead, talk like David.

Now, an intention, of course, is not the whole thing. There must be more. But it's the first step and an essential first step at that. To express your intention out loud—to a friend or a spouse—or to write it down is like drawing a line in the sand. Suddenly, you are accountable. Now it's time to follow through.

Imagine if you had this brief Bible verse tucked away in your brain (because you cared enough to memorize it). Imagine if you developed the habit of reaching for it every time you felt your heart rate spiking when somebody verbally slammed you. What if you said this verse to yourself? Or said it out loud? What if you said it as often as the temptation to lash out came over you? I promise you, *that* kind of self-talk really *will* make a difference.

• • •

SAY IT

"My intent is that my mouth will not offend."

PSALM 17:3

PRAY IT

O Lord, You hear my every word before it is even spoken. David's testimony is true: "Even before there is a word on my tongue, behold, Lord, You know it all" (Psalm 139:4).

O God, You know how I struggle with this. You know the crummy self-talk I have wallowed in up to this point. Would You help me—starting now—to think right, speak right, and love right?

I ask in Christ's name.

Amen.

4

BECAUSE HE DELIGHTED IN ME

He also brought me out into an open place;
He rescued me, because He delighted in me.

PSALM 18:19

Bridgette Ponson and her two small children were walking across the parking lot when it happened. At Layton Christian Academy in Utah, a car whose driver was blinded by the sun struck the family, pushing all three under the car. Bridgette's three-year-old daughter was able to free herself, but not Bridgette or her two-year-old son.

A group of 20 students rushed to the site and joined forces to try to free the remaining two. Working together, they lifted the car just enough for senior airman Dominique Childress to help pull the mom and toddler to safety. Though Brigitte underwent several surgeries, the whole family is now safe and thriving, thanks to the quick action of the students and airman.[1]

There's something about a rescue story that tugs at our hearts like little else can. We never tire of reading, hearing, or watching anything related to rescues. No doubt that's why rescues are the perennial favorites of television and movie producers.

Watching these stories online or on TV, you notice that people will get involved in a rescue for lots of reasons. For some it's a sense of duty. For others it's an act of pity. Still others jump in out of instinct with no thought at all. And, of course, there are paid rescuers—firefighters, paramedics, and the police.

Without question, the most outrageous rescue story in history unfolded when Jesus chose to take our place on the cross, dying for our wrongdoing, our sins. With His rescue, Christ made possible our forgiveness, our ability to live a God-pleasing life, and the guarantee of eternal life with Him in heaven.

Chances are, you're reading this book as someone who believes every word of that last paragraph. But it's amazing how many of us claim to know Christ yet live as if we are unworthy at best—and unloved at worst. Despite the historical fact of Christ's sacrificial gift, in spite of what we call a "personal relationship with Christ," many of us live as if we don't honestly believe we are *that* loved and *that* lovable. Privately, we're not even sure if God wants that much of a relationship with us.

Our self-talk spins wildly into critical and condemning statements like, "You are not the Christian you *should* be. God is not pleased with you—and *you* shouldn't like yourself either!"

What an extreme contrast is David's self-talk in Psalm 18:19. Mulling over God's kindness, David testifies, "He also brought me out into an open place; He rescued me, because He delighted in me." That last phrase invites our further attention.

PONDER THE MIRACLE OF YOUR RESCUE

Before Bob Ross became a cultural phenomenon, PBS aired a weekly show called *The Magic of Oil Painting* with Bill Alexander. I remember watching Bill as he stood before his canvas reminding his viewers, "To show light, we must have dark." Before Christ, there was nothing but darkness in our lives. Biblically speaking...

We were without hope. "Remember that you were at that time separate from Christ, excluded from the people of Israel, and strangers to the covenants of the promise, having no hope and without God in the world" (Ephesians 2:12).

We were children of wrath. "Among them we too all previously lived in the lusts of our flesh, indulging the desires of the flesh and of the mind, and were by nature children of wrath, just as the rest" (Ephesians 2:3).

We were enemies of God. "If while we were enemies we were reconciled to God through the death of His Son, much more, having been reconciled, we shall be saved by His life" (Romans 5:10).

We were held hostage in the domain of darkness. "He rescued us from the domain of darkness and transferred us to the kingdom of His beloved Son" (Colossians 1:13).

We were far away from God. And then came the rescue—and its fantastic achievement outlined in Ephesians 2:13: "In Christ Jesus, you who previously were far away have been brought near by the blood of Christ." That's a lot to think about. But there's more!

PONDER THE REASON FOR YOUR RESCUE

Psalm 18:19 offers this simple explanation: "Because He delighted in me." Used elsewhere in Scripture, this word for *delight* means to please, desire, favor, and take pleasure. Doesn't that blow your mind? Rescuing you was God's desire, pleasing Him and fulfilling His favor.

You're thinking, *What kind of reason is that?* Answer: It's all the reason God needed. And if you aren't already flabbergasted, think further with me.

- God's delight in you is *not past tense.*
- God's delight in you is *not going to end.*
- God's delight in you is *not performance based.*

It is impossible for God to delight in you any more than He already does.

It is impossible for God to delight in you any less. Impossible. Like a gallon-sized ice cream sundae, this good news is almost too much to digest.

Charles Spurgeon looks at this passage and comments, "Believer, sit down, and inwardly digest the instructive sentence now before us, and learn to view the uncaused love of God as the cause of all the lovingkindness of which we are the partakers."[2]

HOW TO MAKE THIS SELF-TALK YOURS

To me, this is a powerful medicine for the soul. So how can we make this self-talk our own?

Choose to Ponder This Verse Regularly

What we hear or think or say repeatedly, we grow to believe. And note that we *do* have a choice. You are the sole gatekeeper for everything that enters your eyes, ears, and mind. This is a verse you want to commit to memory. But don't just work on it until you memorize it. Come back to it again and again.

Choose to Thank God Profusely

His love is profuse. Why shouldn't our thanks be as well? When God has been so generous, how could we be so careless or, worse, stingy? What if you determined that your first waking thought was a prayer of thanks to God for His delight in you?

• • •

SAY IT

"He also brought me out into an open place; He rescued me, because He delighted in me."

PSALM 18:19

PRAY IT

O God!

How can it be that You love me so much?

The idea that You not only tolerate but delight in me is beyond my capacity to understand.

I could never earn it or deserve it, this delight of Yours.

But I want to thank You for it.

Thank You for rescuing me from the domain of darkness and transferring me into the kingdom of Your beloved Son.

And thank You for delighting in me every single day.

What an awesome God You are.

How worthy You are.

How loving and kind and gracious.

Teach me what it means to delight in You, to delight in doing Your will, and to delight in Your plan.

I am delighted with Your delight.

Amen.

5

WHEN YOU'RE ON GOD'S SIDE

By You I can run at a troop of warriors;
and by my God I can leap over a wall.

PSALM 18:29

Who is your favorite action hero? Ethan Hunt, Spider-Man, Wonder Woman, Jack Reacher, Indiana Jones, or Luke Skywalker might be among your choices. So many colorful characters come to mind. But besides being fictional, they all share something in common. They face insurmountable odds and despicable foes, and they are inevitably outnumbered and outgunned. In the novel world, Jack Reacher considers a fight against five enemies a reasonable thing. Yet somehow these heroes manage to prevail every time. They are good guys who fight bad guys and win. That's what makes them heroes.

Things always work out in the end for whatever character Tom Cruise is playing. Same for Angelina Jolie, Dwayne Johnson, Charlize Theron, Lucy Liu, and Mark Wahlberg. But what about you and me? Whether it's *Star Wars* or *your* wars, we inevitably reach a place where we feel outnumbered and outgunned:

- Your adult daughter has turned her back on her faith, and she refuses to let you visit her children lest you "infect" them with the Bible.

- Out of obedience to the Great Commission, you witnessed to somebody at work. Now, the company is threatening legal action against you.

- Not only is the flashing dark spot you see in the corner of your vision *not* going away, but the doctor says you will lose your sight.

- Your car's transmission is in need of repair. But last month, you maxed out on a loan to replace your home's furnace and air conditioner.

Ever notice that there's never been a shortage of trouble? Some days it feels as though our backs are against a stone wall, and before us are troops (or perhaps Stormtroopers?) of warriors. When these moments come, engaging in negative self-talk is almost irresistible: "I'm in over my head and way outnumbered. Loss is inevitable. I might as well give up and duck to avoid the worst of the shrapnel."

David has a word for us. For you. Check out Psalm 18:29, "By You I can run at a troop of warriors; and by my God I can leap over a wall."

Don't you love how gritty this verse is? David is saying that warriors—not a few, but *troops* of them—may well block your path. And don't think you can sneak out the back way either. There is a wall blocking your exit. In other words, you're boxed in. You're going nowhere fast. In fact, you're going nowhere at all unless something supernatural comes along. And it can! *He* can! I'm speaking of God, of course.

We live in an age fascinated with superpowers. Comic conventions teem with costume-wearing would-be superpower heroes. Halloween outfits are dominated by characters with superpowers. Children are even encouraged to dream about all this. If you've listened to their conversations, they almost always begin with "My superpower is…"

While we love seeing imagination unleashed, no one has a true superpower. Some folks are remarkably gifted. Or they have spent an extraordinary amount of time developing a skill or talent to a rarely seen level. But a true-blue superpower? No human is so blessed.

Back to the secret of David's powerful self-talk. Observe that he doesn't say, "By myself," "in my strength," or "thanks to my mental conditioning." He says, "By You I can run at a troop of warriors." God's empowering presence and protection give David the courage and confidence to take on ridiculous odds.

Commentator Alfred Barnes points out that the word *troop* here refers to "bands of soldiers or hosts of enemies." Which means lots and lots of bad guys! Yet despite these overwhelming odds, through the empowerment of God, David goes on offense. Barnes adds, "The idea here is that he had been enabled to rush with violence upon his armed opposers; that is, to overcome them and to secure a victory."[1] Game over!

There's more to this powerful self-talk psalm. David says, "By my God I can leap over a wall." In my junior high years, I routinely cut through someone's backyard to shave ten minutes off my walk to school. It involved scaling a wall on the back of their property. But these neighbors didn't appreciate the many of us who trotted through their yard. So they added a string of barbed wire—which we routinely hopped over. But one day I didn't quite clear that fence, and the barbs tore a large hole in my pants at an embarrassing place. My leg was also a bit scratched. Thus ended the use of that shortcut.

David's testimony is better. He says, "By my God I can leap over a wall." David—as crafty, stealthy, and athletic as he was—does not suggest, "By my skill and cunning, I can hop any wall." Instead, he states, "By my God I can leap over a wall." David seems to be saying,

"Remove God, and you might as well remove the leap. But *with* God, get ready to jump or climb—and win!"

Rushing at a troop of warriors or scaling a challenging wall are amazing feats of endeavor and describe the ultimate fighting force. But the ability to overcome warriors and walls is welded to the empowering presence of the Almighty. Anything and everything supernatural are His. So (and this is no small point) all the *glory* is His.

Extreme dependence *on* God empowers extreme achievements *for* God. But we dare never forget that, ultimately, it is God who does the heavy lifting. This is the kind of self-talk we need.

HOW TO MAKE THIS SELF-TALK YOURS

You face no shortage of enemies. You face no shortage of walls. Your victory is wrapped up entirely in your trust in the Almighty. Say this verse the next time you face warriors or walls you're certain will do you in. Say it out loud. Feel free to shout it! And repeat it as often as you need to, inviting God to do His supernatural work in your life.

• • •

SAY IT

"By You I can run at a troop of warriors;
and by my God, I can leap over a wall."

PSALM 18:29

PRAY IT

Most High God,

You know me for the wimp I often am.

You also know every warrior and wall that stands against me.

I invite Your all-powerful presence in these problems.

You are a wall-breaking, way-making God.

Would You please make a way for me?

And let me be careful—very careful—to celebrate afterward, giving You all the glory for all You have done.

I pray boldly in the name of Jesus.

Amen.

BOASTING—WRONG WAY, RIGHT WAY

Some praise their chariots and some their horses,
but we will praise the name of the LORD, our God.

PSALM 20:7

Nine people were aboard the Sikorsky S-76 helicopter, including pilot Ara Zobayan, who had logged more than 1,200 hours in the chopper. Though the weather that morning was iffy, Zobayan reportedly didn't want to disappoint his passengers.

Taking off into the fog, Zobayan became confused. An AP article claimed that Zobayan "ignored his training."[1] When the pilot thought he was taking the aircraft higher, he was actually descending. Ultimately, they smashed into a fog-shrouded hillside.

National Transportation Safety Board member Michael Graham, commented that as long as helicopter pilots continue flying into clouds without relying on instruments, which requires a high level of training, "a certain percentage aren't going to come out alive.' "[2] Among that sad percentage were basketball superstar Kobe Bryant, his daughter Gianna, and seven others.

That pilot fell victim to the oldest temptation in the world—the deception that comes with trusting in the wrong things. Consider...

- Eve trusted the serpent—and with Adam introduced sin into the world.
- Samson trusted in human strength—and was fooled by Delilah, costing him his sight and freedom.
- Peter trusted in his own character—and denied Christ three times.
- Ananias and Sapphira trusted their clever deceit—and paid for it with their lives.

Nearly every book in the Bible tells of someone whose confidence was misplaced. Mind you, these are often good people—godly, even. But trusting in the wrong things usually leads to disaster.

The aging Abraham no doubt felt he was wise when he trusted his wife's advice to sleep with Hagar to provide an heir for the family. Jonah certainly thought he was wise to save his life when he trusted in a ship sailing for Tarshish. But there's no point in looking back at the trust failures of people in the Bible unless we look at trust issues in our own character.

When our boy, Tim, was a little kid, he was given a model railroad set. I remember spending most of my time putting the train back on the track whenever he played with it. It seemed prone, if not programmed, to fall off.

Aren't we just the same sometimes, spiritually? It's so easy to trust the wrong things. And that leads us to unbiblical self-talk that gets us off track. It often sounds like this: "Grit, guts, and sheer determination will power me through this tough season I'm in. Guaranteed!"

That sounds good. It's the kind of sloganeering you'll find all over Pinterest. But while effort and determination can be good things, apart from Christ they can become ungodly things. So what's a better message?

We find some great biblical self-talk in Psalm 20:7: "Some trust in chariots and some in horses, but we trust in the name of the Lord our God" (ESV).

In Bible times, chariots were fast, armored, and effective. These tanks of antiquity represented the ultimate war machine. Pulled by one or two horses, a chariot usually had a crew of two—a driver and a soldier. The soldier launched javelins and arrows from his mobile platform, rolling stealthily in and out of battle lines. Yet for all their battle-hardened bombast, chariots could not fully protect anyone. Scripture records more than a few chariot-related disasters.

Chariot Disaster #1: No doubt, Sisera felt invincible marching with his force of 900 iron chariots against Israel, as recorded in Judges 4. But verse 15 recounts, "The Lord routed Sisera and all his chariots and all his army with the edge of the sword before Barak; and Sisera got down from his chariot and fled on foot." He trusted in the wrong thing.

Chariot Disaster #2: In a joint military operation with the king of Israel, Jehoshaphat, king of Judah, was struck by an arrow, and 1 Kings 22:35 records that "he died at evening, and the blood from the wound ran into the bottom of the chariot." No doubt Jehoshaphat had trusted in that chariot. But he trusted in the wrong thing.

When all is said and done, what we praise the most, we trust the most. That's why the New American Standard Bible translates this verse slightly differently than the ESV quoted earlier:

"Some praise their chariots and some their horses, but we will praise the name of the Lord, our God."

What do you praise most? That's what you trust most. Have you noticed? Friends who incessantly praise this or that financial investment are showing you what they trust in—money. People who praise their workout routine and their clean diets are usually trusting in their physical bodies.

Something else to chew on. When push comes to shove, what we really trust shows what we really believe. The concepts are welded together.

Chicago's famous 875 North Michigan Avenue Tower features a popular thrill attraction. Eight windows of the landmark building have been replaced with a tilting plexiglass platform. For a sum of money, you can experience what it's like to tilt downward—outside the building—at a height of 1,030 feet. Would you trust the mechanism? If your answer is yes, plunking down your dough is the only way to prove your trust. But going out and telling others about your fabulous experience after the fact would be further evidence of that trust. What we praise the most, we trust the most.

And that takes me to the last phrase of Psalm 20:7, "But we trust in the name of the LORD our God" (ESV). In the Bible, every baby's name has a meaning, something the person was to live up to. Names spoke of family, reputation, and destiny. Names were of inestimable value. In an honor-shame culture like the Middle East, a person's name was their character. Quite a bit different than the cutesy-sounding original names of our day with their convoluted spellings.

When David said, "We trust in the name of the LORD our God," he affirmed God's character, praised His excellence, and utterly relied on His reputation. Isn't that the kind of trust you want?

HOW TO MAKE THIS SELF-TALK YOURS

Next time a challenge comes and you're tempted to say, "I got this," stop! Confess your pride. You're trusting in the wrong thing. Call it what it is, a sin—trusting in self rather than your Savior. But don't stop there. State your unwavering trust in the name of the Lord your God—as you ponder, review, and quote Psalm 20:7.

One last thought. In the Bible, horses represent speed and royalty. As the suffering servant, Christ rode into Jerusalem on a donkey. But when He comes as King, He will ride a white horse. In Revelation 19:11, John records, "I saw heaven opened, and behold, a white horse, and He who sat on it is called Faithful and True, and in righteousness He judges and wages war."

Because our coming King is named *Faithful* and *True*, we can and must trust Him now and forever. Trust Him. Trust Him. Trust Him.

• • •

“SAY IT”

“Some trust in chariots and some in horses,
but we trust in the name of the Lord our God.”

PSALM 20:7 (ESV)

“PRAY IT”

Great God and King!

Forgive me for trusting in me.

I want to trust in the name of the Lord, my God.

I renounce all lesser gods: personal effort, pride, and my spirit of independence.

I acknowledge You now—and forever—as the object of my trust.

Hear me, O God.

Hear me say I trust in the name of the Lord my God.

Amen.

7

FREEDOM FROM NETS

My eyes are continually toward the Lord,
for He will rescue my feet from the net.

PSALM 25:15

Warning: You are about to step on a net. Which is actually a trap. And the scary thing is, you probably can't even see it. That net could delay you, embarrass you, maim you, or even kill you. Worse yet, you may have already put one foot inside that net. Perhaps...

In unchecked anger, you showed your boss what you thought of her—and she showed you the door. Or the flirting at the office led to a hotel rendezvous that has now trashed your marriage.

Maybe your net experience is less dramatic. You have been sober for three months, but earlier today, you caved in—and went to the beer cave. Or, you were minding your own business online when a seductive image popped up. You gave it a click, and it took you where no Christ-follower has any business going.

This is what nets are and do. Hidden from sight, they snag us at an unsuspecting moment, reducing us to pitiful birds locked up in a cage. Ironically, David, the giant-killer, knew well what it meant to be trapped by nets:

- David was trapped by the net of fear when he drooled and faked insanity as a captive of the Philistine King Achish (1 Samuel 21).
- David was trapped by the net of sexual passion when he slept with Bathsheba—another man's wife—and ultimately had her husband killed (2 Samuel 11).
- David was trapped by the net of pacifism when his daughter Tamar was raped by his son Amnon (2 Samuel 13).
- David was trapped by the net of pride and self-reliance when he took an unauthorized census, and 70,000 Israelites died as a result (1 Chronicles 21).

To these nets, add doubt, fear, and jealousy. Though David may have been a man after God's own heart, he spent his share of time in the enemy's own net.

But somewhere in the darkness of those despairing moments, David discovered a secret. It's a secret that turned seemingly irreparable disasters into hope he could hang on to. And he shares that secret with you and me in Psalm 25:15: "My eyes are continually toward the Lord, for He will rescue my feet from the net."

If nets are the problem, what's the solution? How do we talk like David? It begins with grabbing on to four handholds David offers us.

1. WHERE OUR EYES GO, WE GO

Whatever you fixate on is where you tend to end up. In driver's ed training, they tell you to look down the road, out toward the horizon. Why? If you gawk at things just outside the window or in the lane next to you, that's where you tend to steer. Where our eyes go, we go.

Where are your eyes taking you? What holds your gaze day in and day out? Problems at work? Frustrations at home? Inappropriate images on a screen?

That's why David's self-talk here, his determination, is not just helpful but critical. He declares, "My eyes are continually toward the LORD."

2. TO FIX OUR EYES ON THE LORD IS A CHOICE

Fixing your eyes on the Lord is a more difficult choice than you might think. It doesn't come naturally or easily. But it comes with some massive ramifications.

If your eyes are fixed on the Lord, then your day-to-day responsibilities are several notches down. If your eyes are fixed on the Lord, your hobbies and passions (and problems) receive less focus. See how practical this is?

3. TO FIX OUR EYES CONTINUALLY ON THE LORD IS A LIFESTYLE

This is not a one-and-done spiritual gimmick. It's an every-single-day and every-single-hour commitment.

No army that is serious about defending contested territory posts a guard once in a while or for just a few hours a day. If we are not *continually* looking to the Lord, we are almost certainly looking at things that seem important now but may be distracting us from an eternal focus.

4. THE WORLD IS WIRED TO DISTRACT US

In the 1970s, Americans saw only 500 to 1,600 ads per day. Today, the average American sees 4,000 to 10,000 ads daily.[1]

We're also distracted by social media, our screens of all sizes, our hobbies, games, and the latest *ding* on our phones. All that distraction comes with a price tag, spiritually.

No wonder we're warned in 1 John 2:15, "Do not love the world nor the things in the world."

HOW TO MAKE THIS SELF-TALK YOURS

How can we talk like David? The very next time you first sense a temptation to lust, lie, covet, cheat, or cuss out someone, ask yourself, *What is this net?* Meaning what is the actual trap? What is the need behind the temptation? Or what is the real reason you're so angry?

Now quote this verse out loud. Tell God you want to be freed from the net of ____________ (you fill in that blank). If you're still unclear, ask God to show you what the net is—and He will.

• • •

SAY IT

"My eyes are continually toward the LORD,
for He will rescue my feet from the net."

PSALM 25:15

PRAY IT

Lord God,

Would You sensitize my heart to the point where I can feel when temptation has targeted my heart?

Give me the presence of mind to quote this verse aloud. More than that, help me quickly identify the net wrapping itself around my feet.

Would You then please rescue me from that net?

Thank You that You desire victory for me over the nets in my life.

Amen.

8

ON LEVEL GROUND

My feet stand on level ground;
in the great congregation I will praise the Lord.

PSALM 26:12 NIV

Which of the 50 states is the flattest? Many people might assume it's Kansas. But the actual answer may intrigue you. America's flattest state is...Florida! The ground on which sits the house of the mouse is as flat as a mat? It's true. And in the Flattest-State list, Illinois comes in at number two, with North Dakota being the third flattest. As for Kansas, it ranks at number seven.[1]

Globally, some of the flattest nations include Qatar, whose tallest point is a mere 103 meters high. The Bahamas' highest point is only 63 meters off the ground. Vatican City has a height differential of just 42 meters.[2]

At the other end of the spectrum is the tiny nation of Israel, whose highest peak—Mount Hermon—is 9,232 feet tall. One of the biggest takeaways from our first trip there is that the place is indescribably craggy. Those little maps in your Bible that try to show a sense of scale in the Holy Land are not very useful. Why? Using miles or kilometers is only one factor in measuring true distance.

The real challenge of the country is that the terrain is not just hilly but ridiculously—almost raucously—hilly. Only when you hike around Israel do you finally comprehend this. Even though one town might be a mere three miles from another, the travel time might have taken several days for the ancients.

Trying to maneuver around steep hills and avoid sheer drop-offs (while staying in range of scarce water stations) meant that roads were anything but direct. In Israel, there are few places where you can travel as the crow flies. It's the opposite of level.

Just ask Dr. Charlie Dyer and his wife, Kathy. Our two great friends were exploring Gezer's ruins—one of the cities Joshua conquered when moving into the promised land. As the couple was hiking down a dirt pathway in a depression, Kathy slipped on some loose gravel. Her foot twisted at a severe angle, and subsequent X-rays showed she broke her left ankle while also tearing a ligament. Imagine the long flight home!

While the United States has plenty of hills and mountains, not to mention places like Death Valley—America's lowest, hottest, and driest point—we enjoy the benefits of paved roads and level paths, which the ancients did not. We even have safety codes that dictate the uniformity and size of stairs used on our paths.

However, even with OSHA's standards, walking unlevel paths continues to be a problem in our day. At least one law firm suggests the leading cause of slips, trips, and falls is uneven or wet surfaces, contributing to 55 percent of these incidents.[3]

As believers, we have a vague sense that though we know Christ, the cultural ground about us is uneven. It's strangely easy for us to get sucked into fears about tripping. We get tripped up by memories of previous failures and sins. We get tripped up by concerns for the future. We get tripped up by words we've said or didn't say.

We've all got more than a few scars and bruises from falls we've experienced or just feared we would experience. It can get to the point where taking the next step feels like an invitation to pain and misery. If you're like me, you find it easy to engage in negative self-talk. We whisper (or maybe shout) things to ourselves such as: "I've fallen before, so I'll probably fall again. It's inevitable, so I might as well accept it. And there's no way I can even think about praising God in the middle of all this!"

Because he lived in a land—more accurately, in a *lifetime*—of "uneven ground," the calmness of David's self-talk in Psalm 26:12 is actually more of a shout: "My feet stand on level ground. In the great congregation, I will praise the LORD" (NIV). Here is David reminding himself of his reason to praise—"I'm on level ground"—and his reason to live: "I will praise the LORD."

HOW TO MAKE THIS SELF-TALK YOURS

You say, "That's great for David. But I'm not as spiritual as he was. How does someone as weak and ordinary as I am grab hold of this verse and internalize it—to the point it becomes my self-talk?" Three reminders will help us.

Reminder #1

We do not walk alone. In Matthew 28:20, Jesus promised, "Behold I am with you always, to the end of the age." News flash: The age hasn't ended, so Christ is still with us. Let's choose to remember that.

Reminder #2

When we walk with God, He helps to keep us safe. In Isaiah 41:10, God urges us, "Do not fear, for I am with you; do not be afraid, for I am your God. I will strengthen you, I will also help you, I will also uphold you with My righteous right hand."

Reminder #3

When we are certain of the presence and protection of God, we can't help but praise Him. If your praise is stuck on the launch pad, is it possible you need to look up? The absolute, bullet-proof, lifetime guarantee of God's presence and power is fuel for an eternity of praise. So light that rocket and get praising.

• • •

SAY IT

"My feet stand on level ground; in the great congregation I will praise the LORD."

PSALM 26:12 NIV

PRAY IT

O God, I love You!

The certainty of Your presence is food and drink to my starving and thirsty soul. I love walking in the confidence of having You at my side.

O God, thank You!

Thank You that because of Your presence and power, my feet are on level ground even when it doesn't seem that way.

O God, I praise You!

Hear my words, Lord. Ponder my praise. I adore Your always-present company, everlasting love, and never failing power. Be glorified in every inch of every step I take today.

Amen.

9

BIG GOD, SMALL BULLY

The Lord *is my light and my salvation; whom should I fear? The* Lord *is the defense of my life; whom should I dread?*

PSALM 27:1

Bullying. It's a hot topic that never cools off. Bullying at school. Bullying in neighborhoods. Bullying at home. It's become a social contagion as common as a cold.

A Pew Research poll found that nearly half of US teens have been cyberbullied.[1]

Seventy percent of school staff have personally seen bullying take place. Some 62 percent witnessed bullying two or more times in the last month, and 41 percent observed bullying once a week or more.[2]

It's one thing to talk about bullying in schools or bullying as a cultural issue out in the big, wide world, but what about when it's a personal issue? After all, adults are not somehow shielded from bullying. Bullies rarely reach the age of 21 and then magically conclude, "Okay, I've been badgering people long enough. Time to grow up and be a decent human now." Nope. Bullies in youth are usually bullies for life.

Have you ever known a bully? Of course you have. But have you ever met one that wore a neon-yellow sweatshirt with three-inch letters that spell B-U-L-L-Y? Probably not. And that's part of what makes the problem so difficult. Bullies can do what they do, appearing normal and even nice. Or they can be nice sometimes and pure evil the rest of the time.

I have a bully in my life. This person scowls at me angrily and refuses to speak with me. Ever. So there's no way to resolve whatever fuels the rant. I'm honestly not sure what the issue is, but I don't appreciate their bullying tactics.

So, how should we respond? One cynic recommends, "An apple a day keeps the bully away—if you throw hard enough." (Full disclosure—I don't recommend this strategy.) The other thing to avoid is ensuring we aren't needlessly setting ourselves up for bullying.

I'm reminded of the dad whose eight-year-old son dreaded going back to school at the end of the summer for fear the other kids would bully him. The dad tried to console him by saying, "Don't be silly, Someoneyourownsize. Why would anyone pick on you?"

Bad jokes aside, we need to ensure we aren't giving bullies leverage in our lives. But suppose you're struggling with a bully. In that case, you might be so worn down that you've resorted to negative self-talk like this: "My problems—specifically, my problem people—are unstoppable and inevitable. There's no winning with a bully. End of story."

That's one way to look at it: a defeatist look. But what if there were a better approach, perhaps a more biblical self-talk?

Many of us are familiar with Psalm 27. Perhaps we're too familiar, though. Listen carefully to David's self-talk in verse 1: "The LORD is my light and my salvation; whom should I fear? The LORD is the defense of my life; whom should I dread?"

It's refreshing that David doesn't deny the presence of bullies. Nor does he suggest that they are without venom or bite. He focuses, instead, on four "Bully Breakthroughs."

BULLY BREAKTHROUGH #1—BULLIES LOVE DARKNESS, BUT THE LORD IS MY LIGHT

In David's day, light at night was a far cry from the blinding LED flashlights we pack in our pockets today (like the Imalent MS32, which has a maximum output of 200,000 lumens that can reach up to 5,308 feet). Back then, all you had was a small (dim) oil lamp. Hardly enough to illuminate robber-infested roads, dangerous animals, or objects in your path. Darkness was a huge problem. But David says, "The Lord is my light." That's brightness enough to identify any foe or dispel any darkness. The darkness bullies crave is no match for the light that Jesus is. Unlimited lumens. Unlimited light.

BULLY BREAKTHROUGH #2—BULLIES SEEK TO DESTROY, BUT GOD IS MY SALVATION

To the claim that "the Lord is my light," David adds, "and my salvation." We hear the word *salvation* and think of it in a spiritual sense. That may well be part of what David is saying here, but he is most certainly also referring to the idea of rescue. He's stating the bold fact that with God, rescue is always at hand. Because God is our Deliverer, deliverance is always available. Bullies might seek our destruction, but God ensures our salvation.

BULLY BREAKTHROUGH #3—BULLIES ARE ON OFFENSE, BUT GOD IS MY DEFENSE

According to one study, the average weight of a defensive tackle in the NFL is 309 pounds. However, the average weight of a quarterback is 225 pounds.[3] If you're the quarterback, that means at every single snap of the ball, you have guys lunging at you who weigh 37 percent more than you. Wow!

But what if the guys defending the quarterback were all ten-foot-tall and weighed 700 pounds? As a quarterback, you could relax. David invites us to do the same. Why? Because like David, you can (and should) say, "The Lord is the defense of my life." Way bigger or better than any football player.

BULLY BREAKTHROUGH #4—BECAUSE OF GOD, THERE IS NO BULLY I NEED DREAD

David asks, "Whom should I dread?" It's as though he's saying, "In light of all these overwhelming, overpowering odds God's presence brings to my life, who in the world could intimidate me?" No bully can stand up to God's light, God's defense, or God's deliverance. Which means you and I can relax.

HOW TO MAKE THIS SELF-TALK YOURS

It's not enough that this is David's experience, David's track record, David's self-talk. It needs to become *yours*. To keep this practical, let me suggest one stop and two starts.

Stop Replaying

When someone is critical or hateful, we tend to replay their painful words over and over again. This looping soundtrack does nothing to help solve the issue, so hit the stop button. Determine that you are not going to stew in the goo of a bully's blather.

Start Replacing

Negative thoughts have lodged in your brain and need to be replaced, not just removed. Replace those bully blasts with this assuring verse from Psalm 27. Say it out loud. Share it with a friend. Memorize it. Think it. Claim it.

Start Praying

Turn your bully over to God. Ask for His supernatural help and intervention. Pray this verse back to God. Go back to it again and again. It's time to claim your victory by claiming this Scripture.

• • •

SAY IT

"The Lord is my light and my salvation; whom should I fear? The Lord is the defense of my life; whom should I dread?"

PSALM 27:1

PRAY IT

Lord,

Thank You that You are my light.

Thank You that You are my salvation.

Thank You that You are the defense of my life.

Thank You that because of You, there is no one I need fear.

I lean on You, look to You, believe in You, and listen to You more than every other voice.

Amen.

HIDE-AND-SEEK

When You said, "Seek My face,"
my heart said to You, "I shall seek Your face, LORD."

PSALM 27:8

It's played around the world—probably one of the first games you ever learned: Hide-and-Seek. With six grandkids hanging around our house, my wife and I have quickly learned the most foolproof hiding places.

You and I were born to seek Someone eternal, and this passion to seek God is no game. It's scripted into our DNA. As Augustine famously declared, "Thou hast formed us for Thyself, and our hearts are restless till they find rest in Thee."[1]

Nevertheless, many of us do a lot of hiding from God and seek other things *besides* Him. This is particularly true when we have messed up. Here's where our negative self-talk kicks in.

We say things like, "I've blown it again. How can I confess this same stupid sin for the ninety-ninth time and expect God to believe I'm sorry? Shouldn't I be further along in my Christian walk?"

In Psalm 27:8, David offers self-talk that redirects us toward better thinking. David is letting us in on his personal conversation with God: "When You said, 'Seek My face,' my heart said to You, 'I shall seek Your face, LORD.' "

We recognize people by their faces, not their feet or hands, and certainly not their elbows. God is inviting David to know Him—*really* know Him. God is speaking of holy intimacy here.

Consider the typical progression of physical touch in a healthy dating relationship. You begin holding hands. At some point, there might be a hug. Then you kiss.

But imagine how awkward this scene might be: You and your date are out having your first date—dinner at a Mexican restaurant. You just met last week, so you're discovering basic information about each other.

You learn he's an only child. He learns you have three siblings. He's working on his master's degree. You're thinking about changing jobs. Over chips and salsa, you talk about the crazy rainstorm from early this morning, and then—out of the blue—your date reaches up and touches your face—right there in the middle of dinner. This would be considered too intimate, even in a morally permissive culture like ours.

As God extends this invitation, "Seek My face," He invites us to something personal and intimate. We play a baby version of Hide-and-Seek—Peek-a-Boo when infants are just a few months old. Science suggests that even young babies feel validated and loved when others gaze into their tiny faces.[2]

As a dad and now a granddad, I promise you little else is more pleasurable than having a little one seek your face. To lock eyes with a tot, to feel that tiny hand on your face, is an extraordinary pleasure for which there is no equal. Isn't it only logical that as creatures made in the image of God, our heavenly Father feels the same about us?

Isn't it more than likely He gets a particular enjoyment out of locking eyes with us? And isn't it possible He's longing deeply for the press of your hand on His face?

Notice that in replying to God's invitation to seek His face, David didn't say, "My mouth said to you..." Why? Because talk is cheap.

Instead, he replied, "My *heart* said to you…" He's communicating the sincerity of his intent, his genuine desire.

HOW TO MAKE THIS SELF-TALK YOURS

Exactly how do we seek His face?

In the physical world, when we move toward a place of relational intimacy, we:

- spend time sharing
- take time to listen carefully
- invest effort focused on enjoying each other's company

But note carefully that there is no shortcut. This all takes time and togetherness.

Note, further, that you can't do it from a distance—and spiritual distance is always the product of sin. No wonder James 4:8 encourages us, "Come close to God and He will come close to you." But there's no getting close to God while unconfessed sin stands between us and Him. No point in hiding the way Adam and Eve did in the garden after they had sinned.

Instead, God invites us to confess our sins—that is, to agree with Him about them. Let Him forgive you. In Jeremiah 29:13, God encouraged His exiled people through the prophet Jeremiah, promising, "You will seek Me and find Me when you search for Me with all your heart."

When was the last time you lingered in the presence of God? When was the last time you finished telling Him everything on your prayer list and then told Him, "I want You to know I really love You. What's on *Your* heart today, Lord? What would You like me to hear from You?"

Please note: You have to stick around for the answer. You can't just rush off (which is my tendency). Not if your heart's honest desire is time and togetherness.

And what do we find when we seek God's face? Mercy and refuge, among other things. We discover the antidote to our negative self-talk. We uncover a better path for our thoughts and words. Charles Spurgeon commented, "Mercy is the hope of sinners and the refuge of saints. All acceptable petitioners dwell much upon this attribute."[3] In other words, we find hope. Hope for our failures. Hope for our guilt. Hope for our problems.

Couldn't you use more of that? Then why not echo that call of God? Why not say the very same thing David said to God? Go ahead and seek Him. But don't be satisfied looking for a vague cloud of mystery. I dare you to seek God's face—His words, His love, His Holy Spirit's presence. He's asked you to do this. He longs for you to seek His face.

• • •

SAY IT

"When You said, 'Seek My face,' my heart said to You, 'I shall seek Your face, Lord.'"

PSALM 27:8

PRAY IT

Lord,

My culture says, "Seek me!"

My flesh says, "Seek me!"

But Your Word says, "Seek My face."

That's what I want—to seek Your face. Not the culture and not my flesh.

I want to seek Your face more than all these other things.

Would You help me seek Your face today when doubts, debris, and desires cloud the view?

I want to seek Your face.

I choose to seek Your face.

None other is so good and kind.

I love You, Lord.

Amen.

11

DON'T HATE TO WAIT

Wait for the LORD*;*
be strong and let your heart take courage;
yes, wait for the LORD*.*

PSALM 27:14

You might have heard of the "Great American Prayer." It goes like this: "Lord, give me patience. And I want it right now!" There's also a follow-up: "Lord, give me patience. Because if You give me strength, I'm going to need bail money to go with it."

Even those of us who think we are patient...aren't. Banking giant Fifth Third has the proof. They commissioned a survey and discovered that nearly 80 percent of respondents rated themselves as being patient, but in reality:

- 96 percent of those surveyed indicated they will knowingly consume scorching food or drink that burns their mouth; 63 percent do so frequently
- more than half hang up the phone after being on hold for one minute or less
- 71 percent frequently exceed the speed limit to get to their destination faster

- when waiting for a table at a restaurant, nearly a quarter of respondents ages 18 to 24 wait less than one minute before approaching the host again after the wait period has passed[1]

If you're an impatient person (and most of us are), you're not looking for another lecture or well-meaning friend to tell you to stop doing what comes naturally. What you need is a burst of something supernatural. And that's precisely what David offers us in Psalm 27:14.

Before going there, let's come clean. The rotten truth about our impatience is ugly. We blame our impatience on the boss's unrealistic demands, the kids' busy activities, or our excessive commitments at church. There is no question that these are contributing factors. But they aren't the real problem. They're just a cover-up.

This veneer is so thin that we're not even fooling ourselves. Because the truth is, *we* are the problem! It's us! We want the world, the sun, the stars, the kids, the job, the church, the food, and the sex to revolve around *our* wants and needs. We want it all. We want it for ourselves. And we want it now.

Which often leads to sick self-talk. A friend jokingly claims, "I had my patience tested. I'm negative." Another friend claims, "I took a course in speed-waiting. Now I can wait an hour in only ten minutes."

As Christians, we smile and try to sanitize our self-assessment a bit, but we still end up secretly telling ourselves things like, "My life will be a wreck if I wait for God to take action. So it's kind of up to me."

Are you feeling the squeeze right now? As though you're walking blindfolded through the intersection of Deadline and Decision streets? Or maybe for you, that intersection is at the corner of Love and Loss.

You've prayed. You've counseled with other mature believers. But God still hasn't seemed to do anything. You really want to grab the reins and just get it done. And your self-talk keeps repeating that refrain: "My life will be a wreck if I wait for God to take action. So it's kind of up to me."

David has a word for us—*all* of us impatient folks—in Psalm 27:14. It's the self-talk he directed at himself as he rode the merry-go-round of his own unanswered issues. But it might not be the word you were hoping for. He says, "Wait for the Lord; be strong and let your heart take courage; yes, wait for the Lord."

Really, David? Really? I'm already worn out waiting, and you want me to wait longer? It feels counterintuitive, doesn't it? "Just be patient and wait." Isn't that what you were told as a kid? Well, your mom and dad were right. After all, you get the chicken by hatching the egg, not by smashing it open.

But must I wait, David? How will that help? Is there nothing I can do?

Actually, it's not *one* thing but *two*—though let's proceed carefully here. As one wise observer commented, it may be that our hospitals would have fewer pedestrian patients if there were more patient pedestrians.

What is the first thing David advocates? After recommitting yourself to waiting, David says we should first "be strong." The Hebrew words for *be strong* here and elsewhere in Scripture direct us to carry out repairs, become mighty, and collect strength.

If you believe the Bible is true, you have to believe that we are engaged in constant spiritual battles—and war always creates damage. Any chance some of your relationships are a bit frayed? Damaged even? Some repair work needs to be done. What about your daily quiet time with God? You say, "I've been too busy lately," or "I haven't gotten much out of it." Time to make some repairs!

HOW TO MAKE THIS SELF-TALK YOURS

Why not choose to collect strength by memorizing this very verse? If you learn it now, you'll have it for later when your self-talk shouts at you to "Do something!" Imagine calmly but forcefully speaking this wisdom to the screaming doubts that assail you. You've already noticed that I say that a lot in this book. *We must verbally counter the lies of our own self-talk by quoting Scripture.* Why? The Word of God is "living and active, and sharper than any two-edged sword, even penetrating as far as the division of soul and spirit, of both joints and marrow, and able to judge the thoughts and intentions of the heart" (Hebrews 4:12).

Fredrick William Faber says, "We must wait for God, long, meekly, in the wind and wet, in the thunder and lightning, in the cold and the dark. Wait, and he will come. He never comes to those who do not wait."[2]

For whatever reason, it's much more helpful for me to say this verse out loud than to just read it. It's as though I am verbally opposing the negative self-talk coursing through my brain.

Why don't you try that the next time your first instinct is to ram ahead and do something rather than be strong and let your heart take courage by waiting on the Lord.

• • •

SAY IT

"Wait for the L*ORD; be strong and let your heart take courage; yes, wait for the* L*ORD."*

PSALM 27:14

PRAY IT

Lord God Omnipotent—

I want the strength that comes from waiting on You.

But You know my heart, how prone I am to run ahead—and, if necessary, *ram* ahead.

Hear me, Lord.

Help me, Lord.

I commit to being strong—by waiting.

I choose to take courage—not in self, but in my Savior.

Yes, I will wait for the Lord.

Amen.

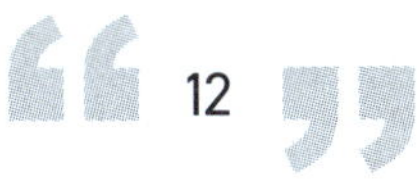

CONSTANT PRAISE

I will bless the Lord *at all times;*
His praise shall continually be in my mouth.

PSALM 34:1

Have you noticed how natural and easy it is to sing praise songs in church on Sundays? The lighting is perfect. The stage is perfect. The sound is perfect. So, praise flows normally and naturally.

But what if one Sunday, you showed up, and the church felt hotter than a sauna, and the auditorium reeked of something rancid? What if your eardrums were repeatedly assaulted with the whiny pitch of microphone feedback, and there were no words on the screen for the songs being sung? How easy would it be to offer your worship then?

In life—not just in church—it's easy to offer praise to God when the lights are bright, the music is in tune, and circumstances are good. But what about when the sour notes come?

When we think of King David, we sometimes think of Goliath (and David holding a sling) or his many other battles with the Philistines (and David holding a sword). We are probably less likely to picture him holding a harp.

We're told that David was "a skillful musician" (1 Samuel 16:18).

But if you've ever tried to play an instrument, you're painfully aware nobody ever became proficient without leaving a long trail of sour notes.

As a kid, I learned to play the French horn, which came at a significant cost in time and effort. But the initial sound was so bad that years later, my parents confided that as I practiced, they often said to each other, "I wish that cow would hurry up and have its calf!"

King David—a master at the harp—endured more than a few sour notes in his life. In fact, he penned Psalm 34 after a harrowing incident in which he was held captive by a treacherous king named Abimelech. After his deliverance, David vowed in Psalm 34:1, "I will bless the Lord at all times; His praise shall continually be in my mouth."

On a Sunday morning, when the lighting is perfect, the stage is perfect, and the music is perfect—that sounds reasonable, nice, and pleasant. But what about all the other times—as in most of life?

I have a strong Christian friend named Rick (not his real name) who has experienced more than his share of discord. When his children were still young, his wife began to exhibit signs of mental struggles. It grew so bad she had to be hospitalized and then institutionalized. Months went by…then years. Sometimes, she grew a bit better and could be released from the mental care facility for a brief time. But inevitably, she had to go back.

Rick lived the majority of his life as a single dad, even though he was married. He did not enjoy the pleasant routine of dinner conversations and quiet walks with the woman he loved. He did not take romantic vacations with her or explore fun new places to dine together.

As Rick and I walked regularly to the train station, I was amazed by his character. He always had a smile. He was always upbeat. He had nothing but kind words and gratitude for his wife, whom he spoke glowingly about as if she were a combination of supermom and supermodel. He praised God and was genuinely thankful for his wife, always believing she might improve.

What a picture of Psalm 34:1, "I will bless the Lord at all times; His praise shall continually be in my mouth."

"But I'm not like Rick," you say. I'm not, either. In fact, my wife has (correctly) observed that I can easily be whiny! And that whining is usually based on a negative self-talk that sounds like this: "Life stinks. I've been ripped off. I don't feel like praising God—so I don't have to." By the way, notice how many *I* statements make up this ugly lyric. Who would want to hear such a song? (Hint: not your spouse—and not your God.)

If that's the wrong song, and the wrong self-talk, what's the right version? It goes like this: "I can choose to praise God even when life around me is falling apart."

You say, "The negative patterns are too ingrained in me. I don't think I can do this." I have news. Rome wasn't built in a day, and neither were your ruts—the ruts of your wrong thinking. Acquiring new habits takes time, but they can be acquired. Like my painful French horn practicing, there might be some sour notes along the way, but if you stay at it, you can make new habits of praise to God.

HOW TO MAKE THIS SELF-TALK YOURS

What kind of strategy do we need to put this into action? Here's what I'm finding helpful in swapping out that damaging old self-talk (quick reminder—I'm very much a work in progress).

First, choose to believe this lifestyle of constant praise is normal and doable. Stop telling yourself it isn't. You are only perpetuating a lie.

Second, tell God you want to live this way. Ask Him for His help. Don't you think He would love to assist you in giving Him what He wants most?

Third—and this is huge—the very next time something rotten happens to you, quote this verse out loud. It will very likely put you in a better mood almost immediately.

Fourth, do this again and again. Answer the next unpleasant thing that comes across your path with this verse. Let it become a lifestyle. As Matthew Henry says, "Be not afraid of saying too much in the praises of God...all the danger is of saying too little."[1]

• • •

SAY IT

"I will bless the LORD at all times;
His praise shall continually be in my mouth."

PSALM 34:1

PRAY IT

O Lord, because You hear every word as well as every thought, You know my tendency to whine. This is not good.

But, Lord, I want to change.

I want to learn to "bless the LORD at all times."

I want Your praise to "continually be in my mouth."

Hear me, Lord. I want this lifestyle—trading whining for praising.

I commit, Lord. The very next rotten thing that happens to me, I will choose to answer with this psalm. I choose to learn this as a lifestyle.

I believe, Lord. You will make sweet music out of my life as I learn to praise You—no matter what.

Amen.

13

BRAG ON GOD, ENCOURAGE OTHERS

My soul will make its boast in the LORD;
the humble will hear it and rejoice.

PSALM 34:2

Your words aren't just yours. Invariably, words and attitudes rub off on other people—for good or ill.

My father loves to tell the story of when I was about four years old, going for a ride in the car with the family. We were stuck at a long traffic light, and when, at last, it turned green, the car ahead of us was painfully sluggish in hitting the accelerator pedal. From the back seat, I burst out, "Hey, get goin', lady!" Apparently, I delivered the line in such a precise manner that it reminded everyone in the car of (well…) Dad himself. As a wise friend once commented, "Most children seldom misquote you. They repeat what you *shouldn't* have said word for word."

Our words and attitudes are not just our own. Inevitably, they impact others. Nowhere is this more evident than life on the web. When my wife and I are booking a hotel, we scour Tripadvisor because we want to know what other people feel about the place we're considering. What was their assessment of the hotel's cleanliness, condition, and location?

Are you looking to replace your car? The smart person grabs as many owner testimonials as possible. And who would possibly buy a vacuum cleaner—or anything—from Amazon without first checking the reviews (as in the words and attitudes of others)? This issue has become so significant that it has given birth to a new industry dedicated to minimizing—or even erasing—negative, fake, or illegal reviews. These firms specialize in sailing through the murky legal waters most of us would fear to navigate—all for creating a good name!

We are enormously influenced for good or evil by the words and attitudes of others. That's certainly true for stock market investors.

But did you ever think your words and attitudes toward God influence others? You heard that right. Your testimony, your experience, and your words of praise or condemnation have the potential to make an enormous impact on someone else.

When it comes to the spiritual life, we have a way of setting this aside, as if it is either false or doesn't matter. Our self-talk often confirms such a stance with ideas like, "My attitudes are my attitudes. My words are my words. My testimony doesn't really impact people around me much."

We say these things hoping to excuse ourselves or distance ourselves from any damage our words and attitudes create. It's as if we've signed our own permission slip: "I hereby grant *me* permission to be as negative as I would like. I further hold myself not responsible for any subsequent damage to others."

Not cool. Not true. Not ever.

By contrast, David says in Psalm 34:2, "My soul will make its boast in the LORD; the humble will hear it and rejoice." As I ponder this verse (and you should definitely ponder it too), three insights jump out at me.

First, when you brag about God, you encourage others. Interestingly, David doesn't say, "Everybody will hear it and rejoice." He says, "The *humble* will hear it." It makes sense when you think about it. Arrogant people don't give a rip about your testimony concerning God or your words affirming what He has done. But don't let that stop you.

Plenty of humble people *will* hear and *will* be pushed toward godliness. The big takeaway here is that you—yes, you!—have an audience. People listen to you and what you say about God, like it or not.

Second, when you brag about God, when you share your testimony about what the Almighty has done for you, others join in. The humble don't just hear with their ears. David assures us they "rejoice." They're joining the worship team, singing the song. But remember, this all began with your decision to "boast in the LORD."

Third, there's a benefit here for which I have no Scripture text—only personal experience. It seems as though every time I follow this biblical self-talk model—every time I choose to deliberately brag about God—I am just plain happy. Others who are smarter than me would probably define that as joy. Call it whatever you want, but it sure feels great every time.

HOW TO MAKE THIS SELF-TALK YOURS

How does this work? How can we move from our negative self-talk to David's self-talk? As I struggle with this issue, here's what I find helpful.

Look for God's Goodness

That might sound like a seventh-grade Sunday school answer, but it's absolutely critical. In a me-first, my-rights culture like ours, choosing to look for God's goodness is an ongoing struggle. If we're going to have something about God to brag about, we'll need to conscientiously look for it. We cannot be entitled and grateful at the same time.

Start Today

Don't wait for a moment when you feel grateful. If you do that, you may never get started. Said William Law, "If any one would tell you the shortest, surest way to all happiness, and all perfection, he must tell you to make it a rule to yourself, to thank and praise God for everything that happens to you."[1]

How to start? Identify something—however small it might be—that you know bears the stamp of God's kindness to you:

- a simple answer to prayer
- a compliment from a boss
- a $20 bill you found in a shirt pocket
- an encouraging email from a friend
- an insight from Scripture that brought you peace

Choose to share your testimony about God's goodness to you with a friend or spouse over dinner. Just spill your story, give God the praise, and watch what happens.

Do It Tomorrow

This is not a one-and-done thing we're talking about here. It's a lifestyle tweak. A change. And that takes repetition over time.

Remember: We *have* never, *will* never, *could* never praise God too much. In fact, John Calvin says, "Men in general praise God in such a manner that He scarcely obtains the tenth part of his due."[2] So let's look for God's goodness, start today, and do it all again tomorrow!

John Calvin also poignantly reminds that "when each recites the personal benefits which he has received, let all be animated unitedly, and in a public manner to give praise to God. We give thanks publicly to God, not only that men may be witnesses of our gratitude, but also that they may follow our example."[3]

• • •

SAY IT

"My soul will make its boast in the Lord;
the humble will hear it and rejoice."

PSALM 34:2

PRAY IT

Lord—

I confess I rarely think about the fact that others are listening to my words and my attitudes. I confess that I rarely think about the thousands of ways You care for me, protect me, and provide for me every single hour of every single day.

Lord—

I want my heart to be a *grateful* heart. More than that, I want to tell others what You have done.

I want Your name to be great, Your deeds to be known. I want the humble to "hear it and rejoice."

Lord—

Teach me this new way of thinking. Teach me this new way of living. I ask in the name of the Waymaker.

Amen.

14

SEEK GOD, FIND ANSWERS

I sought the Lord, and he heard me,
and delivered me from all my fears.

PSALM 34:4 KJV

What is your greatest fear?

Some people are so afraid of dentists that they need anesthesia just to sit in the waiting room. A friend admits to having a fear of elevators, adding quickly that he is "taking steps to avoid them." Another friend was recently diagnosed with a fear of giants. They call it Fee-fi-phobia. Many people fear death less than public speaking. I suppose that means that when they are at a funeral, they would rather be in the casket than have to stand up in front of others and give the eulogy.

Bad puns and jokes aside, fears are real, and we all have some. What are the top five fears people face? Here they are in order: fear of heights, flying, spiders, snakes, and dogs.[1] Further down on the list than most people think—occupying the number ten slot—is fear of public speaking.[2]

Like you, I have my own set of fears. What's on your fear list, and how do you manage it? We know we're supposed to seek God in all our troubles, but do we? Or do we engage in negative self-talk that sounds something like this: "God doesn't seem to hear me when I pray about my fears and other troubles. I give up."

Personally, I find it comforting to know that we are not alone in this business of being afraid. In Psalm 34, David admits to having multiple fears. That caught me off guard. Consider that the one who killed a bear and a lion, the giant-killer, the one who routinely routed Philistine armies—this same David has multiple fears. Then again, how could he not?

Imagine living in Old Testament times. Here's my best shot at creating a list of some of the top fears David would have faced: drought, famine, Philistine invasion, throne rivals, leprosy, fever, staff treachery, wild dogs, snakes, scorpions, bugs, bears, lions…and that's just for starters. While the Bible offers us information about the geopolitical struggles of his day, we know relatively little about David's economic concerns or his family's health issues, but you can bet these were all pressure points too. What I'm trying to say is that David had no shortage of fear factors.

My mother was afraid of many things, including snakes. One summer we were out weeding on the side of the house, and I decided to have some fun at her expense. As we yanked out weed after weed, I created some fictional tale about a television report suggesting this was a particularly bad season for garter snakes—and other snakes as well. As that thought began to simmer, her face darkened with concern.

A few minutes later, I fattened my fib with additional nonsense about invasive poisonous snake species. All the while I kept an eye out for a long, skinny stick. Having found one, I quietly pulled it aside as I waxed on about snakes spotted in our own town. Not long after that, she turned to gather up the weed pile. That's when I tickled the back of her leg with my stick. She screamed. I laughed. And to her credit—she laughed too!

Years later I learned that psychologists call what I was creating for my mother a "sense of potentiation." It means your fear response is amplified if you are already in a state of fear. The bottom line is that even harmless events—like a stick on the back of your leg—seem scary when you are primed for fear. Whoever said that fear is the darkroom where negatives are developed was right.

In Psalm 34:4, David offers us a powerful insight into how he processed his fears—and with great results. With a remarkable economy of words, David testifies simply, "I sought the LORD, and he heard me, and delivered me from all my fears" (KJV). In other words, *poof* went potentiation!

When David says he "sought the LORD," he isn't referring to a quick prayer. The word he uses here means to investigate, search carefully, make inquisition, and seek with the idea of demanding answers. Every single one of those things takes time and focus. I believe David is talking about multiple conversations, extended time with God, and a determination to find answers.

Next David says simply, "He heard me." We should not be surprised. Proverbs 15:29 assures us, "The LORD is far from the wicked, but He hears the prayer of the righteous." On a human level, astounding affirmation and peace comes from knowing we've been heard. How much more so when it is God who tells us He hears us?

HOW TO MAKE THIS SELF-TALK YOURS

The most powerful phrase of this verse for fearful folks like us is David's declaration that God "delivered me from all my fears." The word for *delivered* means to snatch, spare, preserve, recover, rescue. Don't you love every one of those? Isn't this what you want? *I* do!

I have wrestled with an issue in my life that is almost entirely a head problem. This doubt has repeatedly tripped me up, knocked me down, and beaten my soul to a pulp. But I'm experiencing new victories when I swap out my crummy self-talk for this verse in Psalm 34.

Imagine how satisfying it is—on the other side of God's rescue—to say out loud, "I sought the LORD, and he heard me, and delivered me from all my fears."

Why not give it a try? Why not make this verse your own? As always, it helps to memorize it, ponder it, and say it.

• • •

SAY IT

"I sought the Lord, and he heard me,
and delivered me from all my fears."

PSALM 34:4 KJV

PRAY IT

O Lord—

I want this verse to be the story of my life.

You know the long list of doubts and fears and worries that eat at my soul, strangle my peace, and silence my praise.

So here I am, Lord. I want to seek You right now about this: ______________________ (be very specific).

I'm looking for Your deliverance, Your rescue, Your victory. I'm asking You—and expecting You—to deliver me from all my fears.

Would You now work on my behalf? Not because I am worthy, but because *You* are worthy.

Do this thing in me so that I may give You praise and soon shout with David, "I sought the Lord, and he heard me, and delivered me from all my fears."

Amen.

DEPART FROM EVIL

Turn from evil and do good.

PSALM 34:14

The average American moves 11.7 times in their lifetime. According to Census data, about 10 percent of all Americans move every year. Of those, 82.7 percent move within their home state, while 13.4 percent move to a different state, and .36 percent move to a different country.[1] Interesting factoids, but what does that have to do with you?

I have news. God wants you to move! I'm serious. Psalm 34:14 commands us, "Turn from evil and do good." You say, "Jon, I'm not seeing the need to rent a U-Haul here. What's goin' on? Can't I just do a little turning away from some of my smaller sins and call it good?"

What's going on is that you and I are confronted with evil we must turn from every single day. But right here is where many of us stumble. We're tempted to embrace self-talk that sounds like: "I'm not really an evil person, so I don't have to worry about turning from evil."

The Almighty would differ. He's not looking for us to take a slight turn away from evil. He's asking us to pack up and move toward godliness—a neighborhood far away from anything evil.

When the 12 disciples—Jesus' closest friends—asked Him to teach them to pray, Christ's model prayer included the request, "Deliver us from evil" (Matthew 6:13).

Isaiah 64:6 points out, "All of us have become like one who is unclean, and all our righteous deeds are like a filthy garment."

It gets worse. Jeremiah 17:9 bluntly assesses, "The heart is more deceitful than all else and is desperately sick; who can understand it?"

The problem with evil is that not all of it is out there. A lot of it is inside of us. And that capacity for evil remains with us even after we have received Christ as Savior.

Why else does Scripture contain verses such as…

"Love must be free of hypocrisy. Detest what is evil; cling to what is good" (Romans 12:9).

"Not returning evil for evil or insult for insult but giving a blessing instead" (1 Peter 3:9).

Still not convinced evil might be a personal issue for you? Let me put this in a contemporary context. Consider…

- The evil of coveting your neighbor's new SUV.
- The evil of lusting after the attractive worship singers at church.
- The evil of turning a blind eye to a needy neighbor.
- The evil of hurtful words shouted at your spouse.
- The evil of not obeying Christ by sharing the gospel with your coworkers.
- The evil of being stingy in your church and ministry giving.
- The evil of watching a violent or sensual film and feeling strangely comfortable.

- The evil of defending yourself at all costs, including the truth.
- The evil of spending much time streaming but little time praying.

In our decadent digital age, the repertoire of evil has never been more darkly hued or hideous. So what is the right response? Is there a better way to self-talk? Yes! We can opt for this message: "I have evil within me, but because the Holy Spirit lives in me, I can turn from evil and move toward Christ instead."

One of the meanings of the Hebrew word for *turn* or *depart* (used in Psalm 34:14) is behead. You can't get much more permanent than that. It also means to turn off, go aside, decline, leave undone, pluck away, remove, revolt, withdraw, or be without.

Sounds like a fight, right? It is! But what does this better self-talk, this fight against evil, look like in action? It's really about repentance—doing a 180-degree turn away from all this wicked stuff—so you can turn to the good and godly.

I love reading action novels. But recently, as I plowed into the pages of one of my favorite series, I encountered vulgar language and sexual scenes that had no place in the life of a believer. I decided to stop reading the book and get rid of it.

Years ago before the availability of online reviews, my wife and I went to a movie all our friends had raved about. But the film contained a scene where a possessed woman levitated above a bed. We looked at each other and said, "This is not for us." We left the theater—departing evil.

Like you, we enjoy the Olympics. But when the beach volleyball games are played (let's be honest), the girls wear nothing but skimpy bikinis. Watching them does not lead me to godliness. I've had to turn away from this evil too.

I could give you more examples—like our favorite TV detective show. While normally wholesome, the program occasionally veers into darker themes. Once, there was a scene featuring a medium. Bam! We stopped streaming immediately.

Please don't get the idea that I am 100 percent victorious in my struggles. I'm not. I need this verse, this self-talk from David, as much or more than anyone. But this much I know: You and I are engaged in a fight we cannot avoid and must not lose. In the end it's about nothing less than the biblical concept of repentance.

At work, a wellness program pushes you toward a healthier lifestyle. You watch educational videos, do fitness exercises, and observe healthy eating classes. For every course you take, you get points. When you earn enough points, you earn the reward: $20 per month off the insurance cost.

But I've noticed that this is really about repentance. These health experts have the audacity to want me to *repent* from my five-layer Taco Bell burrito. They want me to *repent* from lounging on the couch all evening watching Netflix. Essentially, they want me to "depart from evil and do good."

But here's the truth. I just want the points—the goodies. So I do the bare minimum. I watch the sermons on wellness, but I don't really change. I hear their gospel of good eating, but it doesn't sink in. Which proves I haven't really believed or repented.

What about you? When was the last time you repented from anything?

You say, "I repented when I received Jesus as Savior."

That's great. But because sin is a lifelong battle, repentance is a lifelong work.

HOW TO MAKE THIS SELF-TALK YOURS

Start with repenting. What do you need to repent of today? I have my list, and if you invite the Holy Spirit to show you, you'll have yours.

Evil—we cannot taste it, toy with it, or spend time with it. We must leave it. Totally. The good news is that we can. David's self-talk shows us the way.

• • •

“ SAY IT ”

“Turn from evil and do good.”

PSALM 34:14

“ PRAY IT ”

Holy Father—

You have called me to a fight.

Help me not to grow weary in the struggle. Or complain when it is hard. Or give up when I fail.

Thank You that “greater is He who is in [me] than he who is in the world” (1 John 4:4).

I invite You right now to put Your finger on any issue of evil I have allowed into my life. Be bold! Be loud, lest I fail to hear Your voice.

Let me be quick to own my guilt, confess my sin—and eliminate all evil in my life.

I pray in Jesus’ all-victorious name.

Amen.

16

PEACE AIN'T EASY, SO PURSUE IT

Seek peace and pursue it.

PSALM 34:14

When was the last time you wanted something so badly you would gladly have pleaded, demanded, or even begged for it? Have you ever felt that way about peace? That it's just out of reach?

When I was in high school, our marching band scheduled a trip to Disneyland. Raised in the Chicago suburbs, I'd never been to California, so I was super pumped about going. And then they pulled the plug because not enough students had signed up.

But I wanted this trip so badly that I asked our band director if we were somehow able to get 100 people signed up, would he consider relaunching the trip? His answer was yes. My mission was clear.

I began talking up the trip during band class. My friends and I found Mickey Mouse ears and made Mickey Mouse announcements. We put up posters and drummed up enthusiasm whenever and wherever we could. I even called parents of band students who had not signed up to let them know the trip was "almost certainly a go," so they should "quickly" get on board.

New signatures (and the deposits required to accompany them) trickled in slowly every week. We were at 60, 70, 80, and then 90. When we reached 99 people, our band director signed slot 100 as Mickey Mouse.

The rush that came with meeting the goal after months of pleading and begging is something I'll never forget. And yes, the trip was as great as I'd hoped!

Of course, peace is a much bigger deal than a trip to Disneyland. But at first glance, peace might feel like the warmth of your favorite mug of hot chocolate, a Thomas Kinkade painting of a lighthouse at sunset, or the comforting squeak of a rocking chair on a screened porch.

We perceive peace as pleasant, calming, comforting—and it is. But it's much more significant than that. Real peace—the kind Jesus offers—not only surpasses all understanding, but it's bigger than our misunderstandings too.

But if peace is so great, why is it so hard to find—and even harder to keep? It is said that peace rules the day when peace rules the mind. But that's the very place where most of us struggle. And that struggle is nowhere more evident than in our negative self-talk.

Many of us go through seasons where we feel as though we're failing in almost all of our relationships. Misunderstandings, tension, and conflict rule our hearts rather than peace. I'm often tempted to engage in poor-me self-talk such as, "Peace is something that happens to *others*, but it rarely happens to me. I'm just not good at relationships. Otherwise, I would have peace."

But David offers a different kind of self-talk. In Psalm 34:14, he lays out his strategy: "Seek peace and pursue it."

How badly do you want peace? I'm serious. You need to know that the word David uses for *seek* means to demand, beg, desire, hold, investigate, plead, or require. If we don't want peace that badly, we don't really want it. This means that peace must be:

- more important than the hurt you feel at being left out of the group text...
- more important than the anger you feel over a false accusation...
- more important than the resentment creeping in when someone refuses to apologize...
- more important than the questions you have about why someone doesn't return a favor

This kind of peace has the fragrance of Jesus because it is entirely supernatural. You say, "Sounds great, Jon, but what road do I take to get this personal peace?" The same road David took.

HOW TO MAKE THIS SELF-TALK YOURS

First, we have to seek. But we can't just seek once or twice. The verse says, "Seek peace *and pursue it.*"

I used to regularly interact with a lady at work who was not very likable. This wasn't merely my assessment. It's what other colleagues also observed. Edgy, unfriendly, and loud, she projected an attitude toward everyone and everything. One day I decided it was time to seek peace and pursue it. I went out of my way to say hello, use her name, and smile at her. There was a slight thaw.

Then I learned she had a passion for prison ministry and hosted an annual donation event collecting toothbrushes and other toiletries for the inmates. But her promotional flyer was puny and difficult to read. Would she like some help? She did indeed, so I fired up my computer, designing and printing the posters at my own expense. At this point, things were tangibly better between us. She smiled now.

Months later, I learned she was looking for volunteers to go to a Chicago prison and prepare Thanksgiving meals for inmates. Knowing

I needed to pursue peace, I took a vacation day and helped out. What a difference! By choosing to seek peace and pursue it, God healed the rift between us.

Maybe that story will fire up your own vision to seek peace and pursue it. That would be great, but don't be surprised if you need to return to this verse repeatedly. And don't be afraid to quote it—either silently to yourself or out loud.

I've noticed my relationship issues don't immediately disappear simply because I quote Scripture. But citing this verse reminds me of the heaven-directed mission that is mine—and yours. Think of it as a relational reset button you'll need to press again and again.

Our relationships will never be perfect on this side of heaven. Friendships fracture. Spouses argue. Toddlers bite! Where there are people, there are problems. But just because there are relational storms in your life doesn't mean you can't have peace. You can.

• • •

“SAY IT”

“Seek peace and pursue it.”

PSALM 34:14

“PRAY IT”

Lord—

Teach me what it means to seek peace.

Help me want peace more than winning an argument, making a point, or maintaining my comfort.

Grant me the grace to pursue peace in a way that says peace is more important to me than me.

I seek Your peace, Jesus.

I long for it.

I look for it.

I anticipate it as I pursue peace with all that I am.

In the name of the Prince of Peace.

Amen.

“ 17 ”

WHEN BROKEN AND CRUSHED

The Lord *is near to the brokenhearted*
and saves those who are crushed in spirit.

PSALM 34:18

If it weren't for broken hearts, country music might not exist. If it weren't for broken hearts, daytime dramas would go off the air, romance writers would be twiddling their thumbs, and entire websites would disappear. If it weren't for broken hearts, *People* magazine would have so little to publish that they would have to rename it *People Pamphlet.*

We smile, but it's true, right? And broken hearts are a lot more serious than we sometimes think. The American Heart Association treats broken heart syndrome as a bona fide medical condition:

> Broken heart syndrome may be misdiagnosed as a heart attack because the symptoms and test results are similar. Tests show dramatic changes in rhythm and blood substances that are typical of a heart attack. But unlike a heart attack, there's no evidence of blocked heart arteries. It could be the death of a loved one or a divorce, breakup or physical

> separation, betrayal or romantic rejection. It could even happen after a good shock, like winning the lottery. The bad news: Broken heart syndrome can lead to severe, short-term heart muscle failure. In rare cases, it can be fatal.[1]

Being a follower of God doesn't make you immune from having a broken heart. Just ask David.

When David dropped his harp, dove to the ground, and dodged Saul's javelin, it's a safe bet his heart was broken as he pondered that the king he served sought to take his life. When David learned of the cruel battle death of his closest friend, Jonathan, you know his heart was broken. When David's daughter, Tamar, was raped—by her half-brother Amnon, no less—you can be sure David's heart was broken.

Our hearts are continually broken because we live in a continually broken world populated by continually broken people. The Bible term for all that, of course, is sin.

Yet somewhere along the way, most of us believers pick up the curious notion that following Jesus should somehow inoculate us from experiencing a broken heart. But that certainly doesn't square with our life experience or Scripture itself.

Maybe as you read these words, you feel completely brokenhearted. Is your soul crushed? Your self-talk might be screaming, "God doesn't seem to know or care about my broken heart!" Yet in the core of your being, you know that's not true. What if there was a better way to talk to yourself right now in the middle of your hurt?

David has good news for you: The Lord is near to you. Right now! Check out Psalm 34:18, "The LORD is near to the brokenhearted and saves those who are crushed in spirit."

THE LORD IS NEAR

As he stood in the receiving line after the funeral for his wife, my brother Bob was certainly brokenhearted. The slow, sad parade of huggers and well-wishers went on at length. Bob received them all with kindness and grace.

But after watching him for a while, it seemed cold—even cruel—that he should have to do this alone. Grief is a load too heavy for just one. So I walked over and stood next to him, hoping that maybe a familiar face might be encouraging. I didn't know any of the people, but I knew Bob was in pain. Couldn't I at least be nearby?

Sympathy is two hearts tugging at the same burden. But God does much more than that! He gives us the comfort of His shadow, the warmth of His presence, and the promise that He will save.

Charles Spurgeon said,

> Broken hearts think God is far away—when he is really most near to them; their eyes are closed so that they see not their best friend. Indeed, he is with them, and in them, but they know it not. They run hither and thither, seeking peace in their own works, or in experiences, or in proposals and resolutions—whereas the Lord is near them, and the simple act of faith will reveal him."[2]

Ponder that. God Himself is standing near you. Imagine the power of reminding yourself of this by replacing that hopeless self-talk of yours with "The Lord is near to the brokenhearted." He's near. He's near *you*.

THE LORD SAVES

The second half of David's self-talk reminds us that God "saves those who are crushed in spirit." Are you crushed in spirit? Totally trashed?

One of the reasons I love the Word of God is because Bible people were *real* people like us. And there were a whole lot of crushed-in-spirit folks in Scripture. The Hebrew word for *crushed* can mean collapsed, demolished, destroyed, shattered. Not merely dinged.

Another word for *crushed* is contrite. That's something we need to mind. All the right self-talk in the world won't help us if our hearts are not truly contrite or humble. Let's be careful that in our pain we're not arrogant, blaming God for our troubles while at the same time assuring Him we deserve much better. The Bible offers no promise of aid or comfort for that kind of attitude.

As long as your heart is beating, it is liable to be broken. But that doesn't have to be the theme of your life's script. Oswald Chambers noted, "There is only one being who can satisfy the last aching abyss of the human heart, and that is the Lord Jesus Christ."[3]

HOW TO MAKE THIS SELF-TALK YOURS

You and I can think better and live better. We can choose better self-talk. David shows us the way.

Like you, I've broken my share of dinner plates and water glasses as I've set the table or unloaded the dishwasher. I've noticed I can easily get cut when I clean up the glass fragments on autopilot without reminding myself of the danger in those tiny shards. But when I'm intentional and careful, I rarely have a problem.

Next time you feel the jagged edges of your emotions jabbing you like shards of glass on the kitchen floor, slow down and be intentional. Say this verse to yourself. Say it out loud. And say it again.

• • •

SAY IT

"The Lord is near to the brokenhearted and saves those who are crushed in spirit."

PSALM 34:18

PRAY IT

O Lord—

You know how quickly I jump to self-pity or ingratitude when my heart is broken.

I blame my pain rather than pray to You.

Please forgive me.

Help me, instead, to learn what it means to be contrite.

Thank You that You are near—and not just in a general sense.

Thank You for being near me right now, right in my pain.

I long to sense Your comforting presence.

Thank You for Your nearness, Lord God.

Amen.

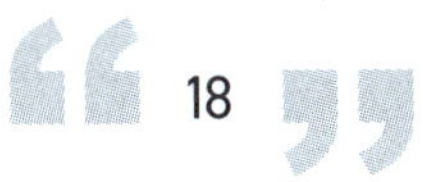

THOROUGHLY DELIGHTED!

Delight yourself in the Lord;
and He will give you the desires of your heart.

PSALM 37:4

You may never have heard of Elmo Shropshire, but you have almost certainly listened to his song, "Grandma Got Run Over by a Reindeer."[1] It's become such a cultural icon that the song was developed into an animated cartoon, and Elmo (naturally) released a sequel album full of other crazy tunes.

One of those sequel songs is titled "Santa Ain't Comin'." The chorus features a group of greedy-sounding boys and girls who demand all kinds of things. Not just more toys, but much more expensive toys.

In response, the Santa in the song announces that this year, he's just not going to show up. He's done!

With respect to the Almighty, I sometimes wonder if He doesn't feel a similar frustration with our gimme-gimme whining so freely expressed in our prayer times.

Given our fabulously wealthy culture, the media monsoon of advertising (as I mentioned in chapter 6, every day we're bombarded with between 4,000 and 10,000 ads), and same-day delivery from Amazon (averaging 368,175 product orders per hour—every hour),[2] it's easy to develop unhealthy attitudes about stuff.

Unless we take steps otherwise, you and I almost inevitably fall into patterns of damaging self-talk such as, "If I want it, God should give it—period. Isn't that what the Bible promises?" And there are so few voices to oppose or correct that wrong thinking that our self-talk gets stronger by the day. "Actually, I've *earned* that cruise!" Or, "Sure, we spend a lot eating out, but we *deserve* it!" This attitude snowballs, ever larger, ever more dangerous.

But the problem is not just the problem. It's what that problem will *become* unless it is checked. Obviously, our culture isn't telling us to pull back. Netflix isn't creating shows that discourage consumerism. I have yet to see a bestseller titled *Be Satisfied with What You Have*. And the undying tentacles of health-and-wealth theology threaten to strangle us even in our own churches.

Charles Wesley understood the danger way back in 1739. Hundreds of years before Amazon Prime, Wesley noted in his journal, "Any unmortified desire which a man allows in will effectually drive and keep Christ out of the heart."[3]

What's the answer? David discovered it. Better than that, he shared it with us in Psalm 37. In particular, verse 4 became the centerpiece of his own self-talk: "Delight yourself in the Lord; and He will give you the desires of your heart."

Self-centered, stuff-saturated folks (like us?) have looked at that verse and sometimes concluded, "There it is! That's God's written approval that I should ask Him for whatever I want and know that He will give it to me. After all, He wants me to be happy, right?" Wrong. On many levels.

David is actually telling us to anchor our love, find our satisfaction, and source our pleasure exclusively in God. Charles Spurgeon does a nice job of explaining it:

> Men who delight in God desire or ask for nothing but what will please God; hence it is safe to give them carte blanche. Their will is subdued to God's will, and now they may have what they will. Our innermost desires are here meant, not our casual wishes...these deep, prayerful, *asking* desires are those to which the promise is made.[4]

The answer is not about shutting off our desires or ceasing to want new experiences. It's about seeing all of life, including our appetites for things and experiences, through the lens of Scripture—in particular, this verse.

TOOLS TO RESHAPE OUR THOUGHTS

Even though I'd never qualify for a job working on a project for HGTV, I love tools. Among my favorites are a laser-equipped circular saw, a cordless impact driver, and the wood-carving tools that my grandpa passed on to me. But you and I need some tools to shape or redirect our desires. So, let's get practical.

HOW TO MAKE THIS SELF-TALK YOURS

Let me suggest three tools we need for the right thoughts.

1. The Tool of Examination

It's incredible (in a wrong way) that you and I tend to give complete, unfettered access to almost any thought that courses through our brains. If a thought shows up, we feel obliged to welcome it, entertain it, and feed it. Not so! Your self-talk needs to speak out: "Hold on a minute! 'Delight yourself in the Lord,' not your urges, wants, and whims." Let's start examining our thoughts, especially our desires. What's really at the core here?

2. The Tool of Submission

If you can comfortably and conscientiously submit your desires to God for His review, you know you're on safe ground. If not, those desires are probably out of bounds. Ask God what He feels about the things you desire. If you ask, He'll give you His take on them. Some folks are wise, and others are…well, otherwise. Don't be a fool. Dare to ask for God's opinion and then submit to it.

3. The Tool of Request

Max Lucado observes, "When we submit to God's plan, we can trust our desires. Our assignment is found at the intersection of God's plan and our pleasures."[5]

If you've examined and submitted your thoughts before God, if you know they are in line with Scripture and seem to be consistent with God's track in your life, ask away! And reach for Psalm 37:4 as you do.

• • •

SAY IT

"Delight yourself in the Lord*; and He will give you the desires of your heart."*

PSALM 37:4

PRAY IT

Lord,

I want to delight myself in You.

But I'm addicted to delighting myself in me—an unholy enslavement to self.

Would You free me from craving myself? My thoughts, my agenda, my desire, my pleasure...they must no longer have my heart.

I want You to have it, Lord—and only You.

Help me take every thought captive, including every single desire.

Fix whatever is broken in the world of my desires.

Then set my heart's desire on You.

For only there is real satisfaction to be found.

I ask in Jesus' freedom-giving name.

Amen.

19

TIME TO UNLOAD

Cast your burden upon the LORD and He will sustain you; He will never allow the righteous to be shaken.

PSALM 55:22

Have you seen the video clip where a man pulls a train weighing 150 tons? Talk about carrying your burdens! But let's get personal because we all have them.

What are your top three burdens right now? I'm not talking about mild irritations or pet peeves. I'm asking you to identify the three pain points that stab your heart by day and stalk your soul at night. Let me suggest a few, and perhaps you'll find some version of yourself or your hurt in this list:

- a boss you can't stand...
- a job you might lose...
- a close friend who is now distant...
- a debt that now drowns you...
- a spouse who's left you...
- an ache that deadens you...
- a cancer that threatens you...

- a prodigal son…
- a prodigal daughter…
- a prodigal you…

Perhaps you often feel as if you're the grand marshal of a perpetual parade of anxieties that marches through the streets of your soul 365 days and nights a year. But I have good news for you. You're not the first to feel this way. You won't be the last. You're not alone.

Still, that good news is never good enough for folks like us—card-carrying members of the "Atlas Anxiety Club: We Carry the Weight of the World on Our Shoulders." Watching the parade of our problems, many of us indulge in self-talk (with an authority not from God) that says, "I must lug around all my problems and stagger under the weight of my burdens." This distortion is particularly true of the troubles we have brought on ourselves through poor habits and choices.

But there's a much bigger, much better offer from our heavenly Father that many of us miss out on day after day. What is it?

David shares it with us in Psalm 55:22, where he invites us to "cast your burden upon the Lord, and He will sustain you; He will never allow the righteous to be shaken." Is that your first response when burdens work their way into your soul?

Forgive me for pointing out the obvious. But please notice that according to this verse, nothing supernatural happens until we cast our burden(s) on the Lord. Nothing is promised or even offered to those who insist on pulling their own train, lugging their own load. We have to cast that burden away first.

But what an offer this is! It's such a deal. We cast…God sustains. Oh, and He even reminds us that with Him carrying our load, there's no need to be shaken.

Don't you hate it when you miss out on a good deal? We all have read stories of lucky people who somehow snagged a round-trip flight to Europe for just 99 bucks. But by the time you found out about it, that (five-minute) flash sale had already flashed.

Missing out on a good deal is no fun. If you have ever experienced the disappointment of letting your unused Kohl's cash expire, you know the feeling. Cleaning out the car's glove compartment, I inevitably find two-for-one dinner coupons we never used—and are now expired. We missed out.

But why would we ever choose to miss out on the life that comes with the powerful self-talk David offers us in Psalm 55:22? "Cast your burden upon the LORD and He will sustain you; He will never allow the righteous to be shaken."

How, then, do we make this personal and apply it to our own world of worries? Thankfully, there's nothing tricky here to learn. Nothing that would demand the knowledge of a lifelong theologian.

I encourage you to stop now and write down your top three burdens in the space provided here:

Burden #1: ________________________________

Burden #2: ________________________________

Burden #3: ________________________________

As you go to your heavenly Father, list these burdens, one by one, and pray something like this:

Lord, I now cast upon You ______________________.
I choose to believe Your promise that You will sustain me in and through this. There is no reason for me to be shaken. Take this burden from me, Lord. Thank You for being strong enough, capable enough, and caring enough. I relinquish not just the burden—but the anxiety that goes with it. In Jesus' name. Amen.

HOW TO MAKE THIS SELF-TALK YOURS

When I quote Psalm 55:22 out loud, I make a huge swinging motion with my arm—as if I'm making the motion of casting something. You might try that yourself.

During a trip to Vietnam, I was fascinated by the hardworking folks who crisscrossed the streets, hauling produce to and from the open markets. Huge baskets were balanced on the shoulders of women and men who moved with astonishing speed despite their burden.

As a curious traveler, I just had to know how heavy those baskets were. So, I dodged some of Hanoi's 5.6 million motorcycles and asked one of the workers if I could trade places. Would he let me try lifting his load? Surprised, he immediately placed the two-basket rig on me, and in an instant I understood the cost of such work—the price their backs were paying to haul this weighty stuff to and from the market.

What price are *you* paying to haul around burdens never intended for your shoulders? Ever thought about that? God has.

When God sent Jesus to Earth to die on the cross for our wrongdoing, He took the burden of our sins from our shoulders. Incredibly, He longs to do more for us. He wants to take the load of every burden off your soul. He's able. He's willing. And as the One who carried a heavy cross, He's also experienced. So let Him.

• • •

SAY IT

"Cast your burden upon the Lord and He will sustain you; He will never allow the righteous to be shaken."

PSALM 55:22

PRAY IT

Heavenly Father—

Forgive me for living so much of life trying to lug my own load of cares and concerns. I cannot, must not, keep going this way.

I want to choose Your plan and Your offer.

Father, would You help me adopt this new lifestyle? It *must* become a lifestyle!

You know all things, including the reality that old habits die hard. So I'm asking for Your help, even though it sounds silly to ask for help in getting rid of something like a burden.

Father, at the first sensation, the first awareness that a burden is weighing me down, would You sustain me? Thus, I need never be shaken.

Thank You for Your extraordinary offer. I receive it now by faith, Father.

In the name of Jesus—who carried the burden of the cross to guarantee me a life free from the burden of sin's power and penalty.

Amen.

20

DON'T FEED THE FEARS!

When I am afraid, I will put my trust in You.

PSALM 56:3

Donna Munson considered the black bears that swarmed across her rural Colorado property her pets. Poking food through a metal fence she built around her porch, Munson fed them, attracting as many as 14 bears at a time, according to neighbors.

One Friday, one of those bears slashed through Donna Munson's fence, dragging her underneath it. The bear then killed and ate Munson. County Sheriff investigator Joel Burk commented, "Donna Munson was dead set on continuing to feed the bears, and unfortunately, she paid the ultimate price."[1]

You may never have fed a bear, but I'm pretty sure you've fed your fears. Probably not deadly—but foolish, nonetheless. And we all have fears: inflation, job insecurity, the wickedness of our culture, the rise of persecution, the erosion of our faith.

As courageous as he was, the giant-killer David certainly had his fears. In Psalm 56, David was in huge trouble. The Philistines—his mortal enemies—had seized him. Now, he was a prisoner in their fifth-largest town.

In the first four verses of this chapter, we discover how David responded to his fears:

> Be gracious to me, God, for a man has trampled upon me; fighting all day long he oppresses me. My enemies have trampled upon me all day long, for they are many who fight proudly against me. When I am afraid, I will put my trust in You. In God, whose word I praise, in God I have put my trust; I shall not be afraid. What can mere mortals do to me? (Psalm 56:1-4).

What can you and I learn from how David handled fear? In this passage, he offers us three empowering truths.

TRUTH #1: FEARS ARE NORMAL

In verse 3, David says, "When I am afraid." Notice that he didn't say, "*If* I am afraid."

The explicit assumption is that we *will* find ourselves in scary situations. So fear is normal. And feeling fear isn't sinful. But *feeding* that fear? *That* is sinful.

What does it mean to feed your fears? It means to fixate on them, to give them a spacious room in your mind, allowing them to freely roam the hallways of your soul all night long. It means to engage endlessly in "What if?" and "What then?" questions.

I've forgotten the sermon but not the illustration. A boy was given a small boa constrictor for a pet. Naturally, he fed it regularly, so the snake grew into adulthood. But one day, whether accidentally or intentionally—authorities could never determine—that constrictor choked the boy to death.

Fears will do the same thing. They start small but can truly choke the life out of us. Fears are unavoidable. But feeding those fears is optional. Don't feed the fears!

TRUTH #2: FEARS DEMAND CHOICES

Verse 3 says, "When I am afraid, I will…" What this really means is—and it's enormous—every fear represents a choice.

Working on this chapter, I faced a deadline—multiple deadlines with multiple projects. Honestly, I felt fearful. But I had a breakthrough one night when I went to my knees and confessed my fear. I poured out my heart to God, asking Him to supply what I lacked. And *immediately* there was a sense of peace even before I'd finished the project.

It began with an act of the will: "When I am afraid, I *will* put my trust in You."

TRUTH #3: FEARS ARE FED OR FOUGHT EVERY TIME YOU ENCOUNTER THEM

Every day—all day—you and I are investing in one of two banks—the Bank of Fear or the Bank of Trust. Every time we coddle our concerns or ponder our panic, we make a deposit in the Bank of Fear. But every time we believe our Bibles and hang on to hope, we are making a deposit in the Bank of Trust.

The Bank of Fear is insured by the FDIC: *Frantic Despair In Control.* The Bank of Trust is insured by a different FDIC: *Father Directly In Control.* Both banks pay dividends. The Bank of Fear pays out doubt, dread, dismay—and more fear! The Bank of Trust pays out peace, joy, hope—and more faith!

Which bank are you choosing to invest in?

HOW TO MAKE THIS SELF-TALK YOURS

When something fearful comes along, say this verse out loud: "When I am afraid, I will put my trust in You." It's remarkably freeing. Try it. The mere act of speaking this verse out loud weakens the stranglehold of your fears.

When the Blast Comes

My family and I visited a small zoo with a black bear whose picture I wanted to take. But in addition to the sturdy chain link fence nearest me, there was also an inner fence that kept us back even farther. Taking pictures of the bears was more like taking pictures of the fences.

But the zookeeper graciously let me inside the first fence—where she stood right beside me and my camera. As the bear approached, the zookeeper shared that she often let the bear sniff her hand through the chain link, but she never, *ever* fed it.

The bear drew closer and closer to the fence. When he snorted, I could feel the blast and smell the breath of that bear! Now, *that* will teach you the definition of fear.

Likewise, at this very moment, you may be feeling a blast of fear as real and as intimidating as a bear. I know this feeling, this smell of terror. But you have a choice. You can feed your fear, or you can feed your faith.

Why not talk like David? Why not feed your faith by trusting God rather than demanding the answer right away? David did it, and so can you.

How Do I Apply This?

It's a safe bet that if you're not already facing a frightening foe, it won't be long until you are: a fractured friendship, the loss of your health, a prodigal child. When that dreaded call or text arrives, resist the urge to let your adrenaline pump run wild.

Go ahead and name your fear very specifically. Somehow, putting a name to that fear moves it from the realm of shadows and darkness out into the light.

Next, quote this verse out loud: "When I am afraid, I will put my trust in You." Admit to God that you feel fearful about ________________, but you want to trust Him in this very moment. Still shaky? Say the verse again. And again. Eventually, David's confidence in God will be *your* confidence.

• • •

SAY IT

"When I am afraid, I will put my trust in You."

PSALM 56:3

PRAY IT

King of heaven's armies,

I not only name my fear but admit my fear. More than that, I want to give You my fear—all of it.

You know my tendency to obsess over this thing.

But I choose now to give it to You and trade my fear for trust. I trust in You, Lord.

Not having an answer yet, I choose to trust in You.

Thank You that there is no need to be afraid.

I trust—and believe.

Amen

21

MOPE OR HOPE

I will cry to God Most High,
to God who accomplishes all things for me.

PSALM 57:2

If you average all 50 states, snow falls across America an average of 28 inches per year. But in the Chicago area, we are blessed with more than half a foot more—try 35 inches.[1]

For years I toughed it out with a snow shovel. But with the arrival of middle age and the encouragement of my wife, I caved in and bought a snowblower. Why didn't anybody tell me they were so much fun?

No need to mix oil or gas for my snowblower. And because it has an electric start, there's no need to yank a rope to beg the thing to get movin'. Blowing all that slushy snow, it does almost all the work for me!

If only life came with a snowblower for the big problems we face. And boy, we have problems, right? Maybe you feel like the guy who complained he had so many problems that he felt like a math book.

I am thinking of the couple shopping for a new sofa. They looked at all kinds of furniture, and the wife reminded the salesman they had a large family. Undaunted, the salesman replied, "I have just the model you need. This sofa here will seat five people without any problems." The husband said, "Where am I going to find five people without any problems?"

The Holmes-Rahe Stress Scale, a list of stressful life events, was developed back in 1967 as a tool to predict illness. And though we all deal with stress somewhat differently, it's tough to argue with this time-tested list:

1. death of a spouse
2. divorce
3. marital separation
4. being incarcerated
5. death of a close family member
6. major personal injury or illness
7. marriage
8. being fired or laid off at work
9. marital reconciliation
10. retirement[2]

Your problem list might be different than mine, but we all have a list, that's for sure. We're messed up, riled up, and stirred up to the point that we look around us and feel cynically that the world has finally achieved "perpetual commotion."

Truthfully, I've experienced plenty of "perpetual commotion" in my life. The question is, how do we respond? Do you mope or hope?

What messages do you send yourself when troubles swarm at you? Our attitudes, if not our actual self-talk, often shout, "I must solve all my problems because it's *all* up to me." This sounds very proud, very American, and very independent. It also sounds like a recipe for lethal stress levels.

David offers us better self-talk in Psalm 57:2. He models this strategy for us: "I will cry to God Most High, to God who accomplishes all things for me."

Do you just cry *about* your problems—the fact that you have so many? Or do you prayerfully cry out to God, *committing* those problems to Him? Those are two very different roads to take.

The first road—crying *about* your problems—leads to whining, complaining, and mega pity parties where no one has any fun. On a physical level, taking this road often leads to stress, ulcers, and heart attacks.

The second road—crying out to God and *giving* Him your problems—leads to a very different destination: peace in the middle of the storm, solutions when there seem to be none, and a way out, courtesy of the Waymaker.

There's something oddly powerful about naming your problems before God. You're admitting your fears, bringing them out of the dark and into the light. And as we cry out to God (intending to let Him handle them), those problems get resolved.

This is easy to write and say but difficult to do consistently. There's so much inside of us that wants to "do the doing"—especially the worrying.

This phrase, "accomplishes all things for me," bears a bit of exploration. Certainly, it can mean to perform, but it also implies thoroughness. When God accomplishes something on our behalf, that thing, that problem comes to an end. It ceases to be a problem. Forever.

Every summer, our backyard (okay, our front yard too) faces an onslaught of Creeping Charlie. If you've never dealt with it, Creeping Charlie is the cockroach of the weed family. Unless you take immediate and ruthless measures, it will multiply almost overnight and infest your entire yard—and the neighbors' too.

Every year I find myself digging it up, spraying it, even ripping it out by the handfuls. And then the problem goes away. For a time. Invariably, it comes back to haunt us—if not that same season, then surely the next.

But when David says God "accomplishes all things for me," he says those problems cease. They come to an end. Lights out.

Time to switch seasons again—it's winter. Remember that snowblower of mine I told you about? It has one other cool feature I failed to mention. It's self-propelled. It literally walks itself down our driveway into the snow! I don't have to do a thing but just follow along behind.

But here's the crazy thing. Instinctively, I clench the snowblower handles tightly and lean my body into its heavy frame as if I'm the one who is doing the pushing and blowing. I just can't seem to let go and let the thing do its job (despite the fact that my grunting and exertion contribute nothing).

Is that ridiculous or what? But isn't it also a sad snapshot of many of us when dealing with our problems?

HOW TO MAKE THIS SELF-TALK YOURS

We like the idea of crying out to God, but we're often unwilling to loosen our grip. I wonder if God sometimes chuckles at us. All He's asking us to do is follow along behind Him.

The movie *What About Bob* includes a pivotal scene when the neurotic Bob Wiley works up the nerve to go sailing on a boat for the first time. Celebrating a triumph over his fears, Bob reveals his secret: "I let the boat do most of the work."[3]

You've reached a fork in the road as you read this book. You can either head left and whine and complain about your problems. Or you can turn right. Turn right into God's presence where you can cry out to "God Most High, to God who accomplishes all things for me." Then, watch in amazement as He accomplishes all things for you.

Oh, and one more thing. Don't forget to follow close behind.

• • •

SAY IT

"I will cry to God Most High, to God who accomplishes all things for me."

PSALM 57:2

PRAY IT

Lord,

Forgive me for whining and complaining instead of taking my problems to You.

Forgive me for insisting on being my own savior when You have already sent Your Son to be my Savior.

I believe You will accomplish all things for me. Help me in my moments of unbelief.

I pray in the name of the only Savior, Jesus Christ, whom I look for and long for.

Amen.

“22”

RELAX—HE DOES THE DOING

My soul, wait in silence for God alone,
for my hope is from Him.

PSALM 62:5

Children are good at many things, but waiting isn't usually one of them.

Sara is one of those smart young moms. When she packed up seven-year-old Jaxon for a three-hour drive to Grandma's, Sara was pretty sure she was prepared for almost anything. Five minutes out of their driveway, Jaxon began the barrage: "Are we there yet, Mommy?" Four minutes later, he asked again. After his third inquiry, Sara said sweetly, "Jaxon, I have a special deal for you. Wanna hear about it?" Jaxon was all ears.

In her sweetest voice, Sara explained that it was going to be a long ride to Grandma's. But if Jaxon stopped asking, "Are we almost there yet," Mommy would give him ten dollars once they got there. However, there was also a flip side. From this point on, every time he asked, Jaxon would need to pay his mother one dollar. When they finally arrived at Grandma's, Jaxon owed his mother $497.

Whether little kids or big kids, we don't like waiting. Waiting makes us antsy. Waiting makes us anxious. We want what we want when we want it. About the only thing worse than waiting is waiting in silence. For folks like us, neither is natural.

But that puts us on a collision course with the God of the universe. Why? Because when the thing you want the most is the thing you need the most—hope itself—you will only find it in the marketplace of the Most High. You can't get it anywhere else. And when you trade in God's economy, He sets the terms and conditions, which are not negotiable.

To some, that might sound like spiritual mumbo jumbo. "Just tell me how to get the hope I need—and fast!" is our cry. But hope is not a Big Mac—and God has no drive-thru lanes. Does that mean there's nothing we can do? Not at all! It simply means we must humble ourselves and pursue hope as God has asked us to pursue it.

We've all been there, nearly starving for a tiny forkful of hope. I know this feeling, and I'm guessing you do too. But when you're short on hope, it's usually because you're up to your eyeballs in hurts, failures, and disappointments. And nothing seems to change, even after seeking God. Typically, in this situation, our unchecked self-talk might sound like this: "What's the point of hoping? My life stinks! I might as well give up."

Though David knew tremendous success in facing insurmountable odds, he also experienced hurt, failure, and disappointment. Despite his wealth and power, he knew what it meant to be hopeless (on the run from his own murderous son).

In Psalm 62:5, he offers us a model for the self-talk we need. He says, "My soul, wait in silence for God alone, for my hope is from Him."

You say, "How does this relate to me, 3,000 years after King David's reign?" After all, you've prepped and prayed but are still worried. Now what? David's advice: Wait in silence.

"That's it? That's the deep, dark secret? C'mon man, there's gotta be more than that!" you protest.

Actually, there isn't. In fact, the more you ponder this verse, the more you see what is almost a theological theorem. To wait in silence for God is to find your hope in Him. Said slightly differently, if you want hope *from* God, you have to wait in silence *for* God.

For people addicted to doing—to clicking and buying and surfing and selling and coming and going—this notion of waiting in silence for God alone is a lifestyle we do not know, a language we do not speak. If you venture on this journey to hope, it's best to bear some caution in mind.

First, the world will offer its own brand of hope under a thousand cheap labels. Labels like achievement, recognition, possessions, money, sex, power, fame, and more. Boil them down; at best, they are merely temporary distractions, a false hope. At worst, they can shipwreck your soul.

Second, waiting—especially in silence—is not particularly fun. In a culture addicted to screens and drowning in entertainment, waiting offers no buzz. So what! Don't be a thrill seeker. Be a *God* seeker.

Third, don't miss the obvious: To wait in silence, you have to *be* silent. But don't go public with this. Perhaps you've noticed that some folks suffer in silence louder than others. Don't be among the loud ones. Most people don't mind suffering in silence as long as they're convinced everyone knows they're doing it. As for you, keep this thing between you and God.

HOW TO MAKE THIS SELF-TALK YOURS

What does this look like practically? How do you do this waiting in silence? Here are three quick ideas.

1. Commit Your Soul

Determine that you want hope badly enough that you are going to wait. In silence. No matter how long it takes. Maybe you need to write this down in your journal. Or put a note on your phone. But start with a bedrock commitment. Draw a line in the sand.

2. Remind Your Soul

Committing isn't enough. This is a marathon, not a sprint. Doubts will whisper at you. Your enemy may scream at you. But this biblical self-talk is more than a match for anything that comes at you. So quote this verse back to every nagging thought.

3. Refresh Your Soul

In the world's most famous psalm, David said of God, "He restores my soul" (23:3). But that restoration is a by-product of letting Him lead us through the green pastures of His living Word while drinking in the quiet waters of prayer. Those are both daily things. We cannot expect refreshment—let alone hope—when taking any other path.

Wait for God.

Be silent before God.

Hope is on the way. God promises it.

• • •

SAY IT

"My soul, wait in silence for God alone, for my hope is from Him."

PSALM 62:5

PRAY IT

Lord God of heaven—

I affirm that You are the Source of all hope.

Apart from You, outside of You, it does not exist.

Hope is found only in Your person, and only by calling on Your name, living in Your words and ways, will I find it.

I commit now to waiting in silence for You alone.

I will remind myself of this truth as often as lies come along to challenge me.

I will refresh myself daily in Your Word and in prayer.

Thank You for the certainty of Your hope.

Amen.

“ 23 ”

WHO IS YOUR ROCK?

He alone is my rock and my salvation, my refuge; I will not be shaken...Trust in Him at all times, you people; pour out your hearts before Him; God is a refuge for us.

PSALM 62:6, 8

As she peered out the hospital window, clouds turned into claws and trees began to tremble. Dory knew she needed to head home before the worst of the storm arrived. It was time to leave her husband in the care of the doctors. Not easily done. He'd had a heart attack just five days earlier.

Gripping the steering wheel of her Chevy, Dory hoped she would make it home before the worst of the Arkansas storm hit. At about 6:30 she turned onto her driveway and then hurried inside to put some meat in a frying pan for dinner. At 6:55 p.m., Dory's watch stopped. That's when her house exploded. A tornado had struck.

Their car was buried under the rubble of what was once a beautiful fireplace.

Their refrigerator was blown nearly 200 feet across the road into a gully, where it sat upright. One hinge was broken but inside was an egg carton with one fresh egg unbroken. They also found the frying pan with the meat still in it. Dory's clothes were scattered throughout the forest, and one of her quilts was later found across the lake in a tree.

As for Dory, the tornado lifted her above 50-foot trees. Ultimately, she was thrown a thousand feet into the forest. When a search party finally heard her whimper, they rushed her to the hospital.

The attending physician—the same doctor who had cared for her husband—later announced that despite his team's best efforts, Dory's internal injuries were too many to overcome. She was not yet 60.

Dory was my grandmother. The real tragedy of the story is that though her home had a basement, she could only access it from outside. Given the speed at which the tornado swept through the neighborhood, she simply could not get to a place of refuge in time.

While few of us will ever encounter a tornado like that, we all face storms of our own—sometimes of our own making:

- storms of unemployment
- storms of divorce
- storms of death
- storms of sickness

Inevitably, storms leave behind a trail of loss and destruction. And once you've had the unpleasant task of sifting through the wreckage, it's easy to develop a sense of astraphobia—an intense fear of storms.

As a coping mechanism, many of us respond by engaging in negative self-talk every time the slightest hint of a storm presents itself. If we're honest, we'll admit to expressing thoughts like, "Deep inside, I am afraid because nothing and no one is entirely reliable." And this becomes our dominant self-talk. At the first rumble, the faintest flash of lightning, we assume an emotional version of the fetal position.

As you read Scripture, you realize there was rarely a chapter in David's life without a storm. In fact, he sometimes faced storms within storms. For David, storms were the norm. For us too.

How did David reply to his gnawing fears, the nasty whispers suggesting that maybe there *wasn't* a refuge for him anywhere? What self-talk insights does he offer us?

His answer is found in Psalm 62:6, 8. Testifying to God's unfailing provision, David proclaims, "He alone is my rock and my salvation, my refuge; I will not be shaken...Trust in Him at all times, you people; pour out your hearts before Him; God is a refuge for us."

David gives us a three-point strategy toward better self-talk in this brief passage. Listen to his storm survival strategy. It's amazingly practical.

First, in verse 6, David essentially says, "I remind myself that my salvation rests exclusively on God." If our salvation is going to rest "exclusively on God," it cannot rest on anything or anyone else. This means we forcefully reject all other voices. Just as marriage implies an exclusive relationship, so does our trust relationship with God. He will not be one refuge among many. He will not be satisfied with being on your top ten list. David says, "He alone is my rock and my salvation." With God as your rock and your salvation, you and your future are completely secure! Worrying in the face of God is ridiculous. David says, "I will not be shaken." You can say that too.

In verse eight, David's second strategy is, "Trust in Him at all times, you people; pour out your hearts before Him." Consider this. The Creator of the universe invites you to trust in Him even as you pour out your heart before Him. Somewhere along the way, I think many of us start believing a hideous lie—that God is somehow less than interested in hearing from us, especially our fears. We reason that we should be further along in our spiritual journey, and God must be weary of—if not angry at—us and our unending fears. Yet He who extends this invitation is the one who invites us to cry out to Him as Abba Father—Daddy!

David's third strategy for storm survival is His constant calling to mind that God is his refuge. Three times in three verses, he reminds himself that God—and God alone—is his refuge. David writes it, speaks it, and (given the fact that he is a musician of renown) sings it. "God is my refuge" is a theme David comes back to again and again. If *he* needed those regular reminders, so do we.

HOW TO MAKE THIS SELF-TALK YOURS

I wish I could promise you sunny weather every hour of every day for the rest of your life, but I can't. It's probably much truer that a storm of some kind is headed your way. What will you do then? Resort to feeble ways of negative self-talk? I hope not.

Instead, I invite you right now to choose to turn to God alone as your rock. I invite you to pour out your heart to Him, holding nothing back. And I invite you to remind yourself, as often as needed, that God is your Refuge. You can't say it too much or come to Him too frequently. Go to your Refuge now. He's waiting for you.

• • •

SAY IT

"He alone is my rock and my salvation, my refuge; I will not be shaken...Trust in Him at all times, you people; pour out your hearts before Him; God is a refuge for us."

PSALM 62:6, 8

PRAY IT

Most High God—

I praise You that You are my Rock, my Refuge.

Thank You that You sent Jesus, who walked on storm-tossed water.

Thank You that He still walks on and through the storms of our lives.

Thank You for Your plain invitation to pour out my heart before You.

You are the rock of my strength, my Refuge.

You, Lord, are the exclusive source of my hope and help—and I want no other.

Thank You that You will see me through this storm—and the next and the next and the next—until, at last, You take me to the shores of the crystal sea where storms are no more and life never ends.

Amen.

24

A HOME FOR THE EMOTIONALLY HOMELESS

God makes a home for the lonely;
He leads out the prisoners into prosperity,
only the rebellious live in parched lands.

PSALM 68:6

According to the United States Census Bureau, one out of every thousand Americans lives in a shelter for the homeless.[1] For lots of reasons, more people than ever are experiencing homelessness and its accompanying loneliness for the first time. That's bad enough.

But what if there were a way to measure how many of us feel *emotionally* homeless, lonely, and disconnected from everyone? And what about those who feel spiritually homeless, convinced that God doesn't really know or care about them? What might those numbers look like?

According to a poll by the American Psychiatric Association, about one in three US adults say they feel lonely at least once a week. And one in ten Americans now say they feel lonely every day. Sadly, 13 percent use drugs or alcohol to ease their loneliness.[2]

Unsurprisingly, all this loneliness takes a toll on our health. A study from the National Library of Medicine suggests poor social relationships (characterized by social isolation or loneliness) were associated with a 29 percent increased risk of heart disease and a 32 percent increased risk of stroke. Loneliness was also associated with higher rates of depression, anxiety, and suicide.[3]

Mother Teresa was apparently not far off the mark when she said, "The world's greatest disease is loneliness."[4]

Everyone feels lonely from time to time, but that's different from being chronically lonely. When loneliness moves in and takes up residence in your heart, marching up and down the hallways of your soul, it's a whole different story. Our degraded self-talk shouts into those echoey hallways, "I'm lonely and feel emotionally homeless—and that's how it always will be!"

We sometimes feel as destitute as the guy who signed up to join a loneliness therapy group—but nobody showed up. Is that the end of the story? Are we destined for a life of loneliness? Must loneliness have the last word?

Short answer: Not unless you allow it to. Just ask David. Tending the sheep, hiding from Saul, hunting the Philistines, fleeing from Absalom—David knew loneliness. In fact, if the School of Hard Knocks awarded diplomas for enduring loneliness, David could have wallpapered his palace with the certificates.

However, although David experienced loneliness, he refused to be defined by it. In Psalm 68, he offers us a glimpse into his own self-talk. In verse 6, David writes, "God makes a home for the lonely; He leads out the prisoners into prosperity, only the rebellious live in parched lands."

By the way, scholars believe this particular psalm—a hymn—was written when the ark of the covenant was finally returned from exile to its rightful place in Jerusalem. You can read the story in 2 Samuel 6. My point is two-fold. First, we can't pluck verses out of the Psalms (or any Bible passage) randomly without considering their context. Second, it strikes me as ironic that as the ark is returned to its home, David chooses to write about God's provision of a home for the lonely.

Here are three powerful considerations to ponder as we consider God's offer of a home for the lonely.

1. WHAT GOD MAKES, HE MAKES WELL

Has God ever created a dud? Have the constellations ever been *less* than stellar? Is the Grand Canyon ever *not* grand? Has anything God made ever worn out, fallen apart, or rusted through? Of course not. That means the home our moon-making, sunset-painting God offers you is truly awesome, something worth living for and in.

2. GOD IS ALWAYS HOME IN HIS HOME

That means you never need to be lonely. Quite literally, you are never, ever alone. In Psalm 139:7, David asks, "Where can I go from Your Spirit? Or where can I flee from Your presence?" The obvious answer is nowhere.

As if that isn't exciting enough, consider that no one can take this home away from you. Notice that no fine print or performance clause is in this passage. You don't get evicted for late payments (there are none). God is always at home. So you don't ever have to be alone.

3. WHAT GOD MAKES, ONLY GOD CAN GIVE

Because God makes the home, He controls who gets to live there. We don't get this home through any effort of our own. We don't get it by reading enough self-help books or attending enough therapy sessions.

In John 14, Jesus talked about the home He was preparing for His followers—and the way to find that home. In verse 6, He said, "I am the way, and the truth, and the life; no one comes to the Father except through Me."

In other words, if you want this ultimate home—peace in this life and eternal life with Christ—you must first come to Him. You acknowledge that you have messed up (we're all sinners). Then you ask Christ to forgive you and take charge of your life—to be your Savior. Have you done that? If not, this is your moment. Do it now.

> *Father, I come to You now the way You asked me to come—through Jesus. I believe He died on the cross to pay for my wrongdoing. I ask You to forgive me of all my sins. Please be in charge of my life from this day forward, my Savior. I look forward to enjoying the home You have for me—in this life and the life to come. Amen.*

HOW TO MAKE THIS SELF-TALK YOURS

The next time you feel an icy wave of loneliness dumping all over you, piercing you with the chill of its numbing negativity, speak this verse out loud. Tell yourself the truth: "God makes a home for the lonely." Challenge the echoey condemnation of your fears. They are really just lies, you know. Answer them all—every last one of them—with this outstanding promise from your Maker: God makes a home for the lonely.

• • •

SAY IT

"God makes a home for the lonely; He leads out the prisoners into prosperity, only the rebellious live in parched lands."

PSALM 68:6

PRAY IT

Father,

Thank You for Your promise of a home.

Thank You for letting me know that even though I sometimes feel lonely, I am not alone in Your home. Not now. Not ever.

Thank You for inviting me to live in the shelter of the Most High God. I choose to stay there.

With You. At home.

Amen.

THE EVERYDAY BURDEN-BEARER

Blessed be the Lord, who daily bears our burden,
the God who is our salvation.

PSALM 68:19

It's been a weird life.

To date, my wife and I have traveled to 41 countries—many of them repeatedly. Typically, those trips are built around media acquisition. I'm recording audio interviews or video testimonials, or I'm shooting photos while writing blogs and articles.

Even in our digital age, the equipment required is significant: camera, lenses, digital audio recorder, microphones, cables, lights, tripods, batteries, chargers, and electrical adapters—not to mention my trusty iPad and its Bluetooth keyboard. And don't forget the snacks!

Everything is crammed into a beefy backpack that ends up weighing more than 30 pounds. Surprisingly, all that weight is distributed nicely over the shoulders, and it hardly slows me down.

But I've noticed that after traveling overseas for a week or two—lugging that hefty weight day after day—once I get home and switch to my usual (smaller and lighter) backpack, it feels odd. Honestly, not being weighed down feels...well, not right. Apparently, I've become used to bearing my burden.

But you don't need a passport or plane ticket to some faraway country to know what it means to bear a heavy burden. In the grind of life, most of us become so used to lugging burdens (heavy burdens)—*lots* of burdens—that we don't feel normal without them. And because you've lived a while, you know that the heaviest backpacks and physical burdens are nothing compared to the emotional and psychological burdens many of us carry around.

We stash these burdens in a backpack that becomes heavier and heavier—never lighter. And toting it around is a task for which we were never built. If only there were some relief.

Good news—there is!

Bad news—relief often evades us! Why?

Somewhere in the twisted maze of our minds, we get the idea that God is weary or unhappy in His self-appointed role of helping us. Is it pride on our part? A quest for self-sufficiency (also pride)? Whatever the label, we often don't like admitting we have needs and, at the same time, we wonder if God even wants to bother with them.

In our heaviest moments, our warped self-talk whispers, "God is tired of me asking for His assistance. He helps sometimes but has more important things to do than mess with my messes." Not only is that not true, but it's also ridiculous!

Fortunately for us, David learned better self-talk. He discovered that even a mighty king with power, wealth, and wisdom needed someone to carry his burdens. In Psalm 68:19, he testifies, "Blessed be the Lord, who daily bears our burden, the God who is our salvation." The same God who saved you longs to bear your burdens—the very ones you think He doesn't care about.

Both of our firstborn grandkids share the same personality trait—a drive for independence. As tots, we often asked them, "Would you like some help with that?" Invariably the response was, "I do it!"

Most of us are the same as adults. We have an enormous desire to be independent, self-sustaining, and on our own. Even in the face of divorce or death, we maintain a stiff upper lip and try to shoulder the entire load of our burdens.

How silly. It's a role we were never intended to fill. Trying to play God is not only ineffective but also exhausting. Consider what David is saying here. His better self-talk reminds us that with God, burden-bearing is not merely a hobby. It's a passion, something He delights to do. Lifting the weight off our shoulders is in God's DNA. He never grows tired, never grows tired of us, never grows tired of daily lifting our burdens.

That means tomorrow, He'll be just as ready, willing, and enthused to lift your burdens as today. And the next day. And the next day. Hardly a day goes by without some new burden dumping all over you. Isn't that true? But the verse says, He *daily* bears our burdens.

What are your burdens right now? The top three? God promises to bear them, to do the heavy lifting for us. But how does this work? How can you "let go and let God," as the old bumper sticker used to proclaim?

If you've ever shopped at an IKEA store, you've likely marveled at the escalator system. Running parallel to the usual escalator for people is one designated exclusively for shopping carts. You and your family ride up or down without lugging or shoving your heavily laden shopping cart. Its wheels click into a gearing system that moves the whole load for you. All you have to do is enjoy the ride! However, I must confess that this system is so different from what I'm used to that every time I stare at that cart, a small part of me tenses up and wonders if I should be doing something. I just can't seem to let go and let the escalator do its job.

Ridiculous? Sure. But isn't that also a snapshot of many of us when it comes to dealing with our problems? We like the idea of crying out to God, but we're often unwilling to loosen our grip. I wonder if God chuckles at us. All He's asking us to do is follow along behind Him while He does the work.

HOW TO MAKE THIS SELF-TALK YOURS

In the end, this is an everyday thing. Why? There's not much benefit in visiting the King once in a while. If we would have God *daily* bear our burdens, we must *daily* be in contact with Him. Daily in prayer, daily in Scripture reading, daily in telling Him about our burdens.

God is your daily burden-bearer whether you choose Him to be so or not. Why not let Him do what He does best? What only *He* can do? Why not let Him be *your* daily burden-bearer? Start today. Here's how:

1. Name your burdens—all of them. Write them down if you must, or speak them out loud. But name them all.
2. Invite God to bear them for you. Tell Him you're weary of carrying the load. Ask Him to show you His strength and grace.
3. Repeat this process daily, quoting Psalm 68:19. Consider memorizing this verse.

I promise, over time, you'll see a difference. David did, and so will you.

• • •

SAY IT

"Blessed be the Lord, who daily bears our burden, the God who is our salvation."

PSALM 68:19

PRAY IT

Heavenly Father,

Thank You for really caring!

I face burdens every day.

But I affirm that You are more than able to handle them.

At this very moment, the heaviest burden I am facing is ________________________.

I invite You to bear this for me. It's too much for me, Father.

Thank You for being my everyday Burden-Bearer.

I look forward to the way You will lead in my life.

Amen.

26

ESCAPE FROM DEATH—YOURS!

God is to us a God of salvation; and to GOD the Lord belong ways of escape from death.

PSALM 68:20

Ours is a culture obsessed with safety. Safety stickers, signs, posters, and more warn us of danger and death at every turn. Online and on television, fine print and rapid-fire voice-overs practically shout safety messages at us—some of which are almost comical.

A popular hair dryer maker warns, "Do not use while sleeping." At home, our new washing machine warns, "Do not put any person in this washing machine." (I'm not joking.) I saw a sticker on a New Holland Tractor urging me to "Avoid Death."

But despite all the warnings, we still die. The numbers vary, but somewhere around 8,000 Americans die every day. According to the Centers for Disease Control, here are the top eight causes—in order:

1. heart disease
2. cancer
3. accidents
4. stroke

5. respiratory diseases
6. Alzheimer's disease
7. diabetes
8. kidney disease[1]

The National Safety Council estimated 44,450 people died in traffic crashes in 2023. And with more drivers on the road since then, it's a safe bet those numbers will continue to climb.[2]

In fact, the Association for Safe International Road Travel (ASIRT) reports that road traffic injuries are the leading cause of death among people aged five to twenty-nine.[3]

This caused one cynical friend to comment, "The number one need in car safety today is the recall of several million drivers! And the most effective safety measure in the automotive world might be accidentally locking their keys inside the car."

With lawyers waxing and common sense waning, individual responsibility is vanishing. And that can lead to more deaths.

Then, too, we must acknowledge that there is no shortage of dangers in our world. Indeed, the "Lexicon of Lethality" has never been so varied. Electric cars are terrific, but when they spontaneously combust after being flooded—that's dangerous. A wade in the ocean is refreshing. Awash in the ocean, we're dead. A fire in the fireplace is lovely. But out of control, fire is lethal. Doctor-prescribed drugs are a blessing. But abused, they become killers.

You get the point. The danger is everywhere.

- biological weapons
- nuclear bombs
- land mines
- power grid failure

The possibility of death is increasing. Although we have technology that previous generations did not have, death has always been a threat—and a fear.

Luckily for us, we don't normally face the threat of death from bears, lions, jackals, and wild dogs. But David did. And, of course, his generation had none of the lifesaving surgeries and drugs we enjoy today. My point is simply that death—of all kinds—has always been something to fear. And that makes deliverance a huge deal.

But our fears of death are much bigger than merely physical. We fear the death of our relationships, our reputations, our job security, our financial well-being. We fear the death of rapport with our kids and grandkids. We fear the death of our freedoms. The list is practically limitless—and so are our fears.

Many of us reasonably manage our doomsday fears, but some of us are so taken in that we become almost paralyzed. Whether the death of a dream, the death of a friendship, or a literal impending death, we gravitate toward negative self-talk. Our self-talk often descends to depths such as: "The struggle I am facing now will be the death of my reputation...relationship... employment...or financial well-being. There's no way out. I might as well give up on ______________."

The fact is, you've already survived several of these "certain death" experiences we're talking about. In your head, you know that your self-talk is neither true nor helpful. What if you could trade all that in for a better brand of self-talk? Where to get it?

Check out Psalm 68:20. It says, "God is to us a God of salvation, and to God the Lord belong ways of escape from death."

Our tendency is to look at this verse with our New Testament-tinted glasses and assume this is primarily a reference to God's plan for redeeming lost men and women through the death of Christ. While the verse makes sense in that framework, remember that David lived a thousand years before Christ. Note further that the Hebrew word for *salvation* also means deliverance. So here, David is speaking about God's role as Deliverer from difficulties and deaths—of all kinds.

Charles Spurgeon looked at this passage and commented, "The Almighty who has entered into covenant with us is the source of our safety, and the author of our deliverances."[4] Note Spurgeon's use of the plural here: deliverances.

You and I are trouble prone, disaster bound, and in constant need of rescue. That's why God stands ready for any and all deliverances. No wonder one of His names is Waymaker!

HOW TO MAKE THIS SELF-TALK YOURS

How can we make this verse a victory verse? How can we learn to use this biblical self-talk? Here are three quick ideas.

1. Tell God What You Need

Yes, He already knows, but for whatever reason, He has asked us (commanded us) to "let your requests be made known to God" (Philippians 4:6).

2. Ask for His Deliverance

Again, God loves to hear us ask for His help. So be bold and be specific. Isaiah 30:18 assures us that "the Lord longs to be gracious to you, and therefore He waits on high to have compassion on you."

3. Speak Truth to Your Doubts

Not just any truth—speak the truth of Psalm 68:20. This fight against fear—especially the fear of death—is never a one-and-done proposition. Doubts and fears will come at you again and again. You must answer every one of those lies with the truth.

One last thought—and this one is from Spurgeon again. He assures us, "As surely as he is our God, he will save us. To be his is to be safe."[5]

• • •

SAY IT

"God is to us a God of salvation; and to GOD *the Lord belong ways of escape from death."*

PSALM 68:20

PRAY IT

God of my salvation—

I praise You for Your work of deliverance.

Not a once-in-a-while thing, but an everyday thing.

I ask You now to deliver me from ____________________.

You have delivered me in the past.

You are delivering me in the present.

You will deliver me safely every day until the end of this earthly life and the beginning of that better life—the life without end.

Thank You for making this possible through the death and resurrection of our Waymaker, Christ Jesus.

Amen.

SAY IT AGAIN. AND AGAIN!

May those who love Your salvation say continually, "May God be exalted!"

PSALM 70:4

Are you stingy?

J. Paul Getty was reportedly the world's first billionaire. Though he owned a 70-room house outside of London, he reportedly installed a coin-operated pay phone for his guests. Worse, he complained to his (fifth) wife, Louise, that she spent way too much money on medical care for their blind six-year-old son, Timmy.

In 1973, Getty's eldest grandson, 16-year-old Paul, was kidnapped in Rome and held for five months for ransom by the Calabrian Mafia. To show Getty they meant business, they sliced off the boy's right ear and sent it to a newspaper, saying the rest of him would arrive "in little bits" unless the ransom was paid. Believe it or not, Getty haggled the ransom amount down from $14 million to $3.2. Ultimately, he only paid $2.2 million, loaning his son the rest of the money—at 4 percent interest.[1]

Most of us aren't anywhere near that stingy. We're just...well, economical in a rather obnoxious way. Some of us, though, are as tight as a submarine door.

Truthfully, we're all stingy in some areas. Some of us are great at giving to church but lousy at spending on our families. Others might share their money but will hardly give you a minute of their time. Still others are generous with their families but stingy toward ministries.

But what about the way we relate to God? Are we stingy toward our Creator? I'm not speaking in financial terms. I'm talking about stinginess in a way that means much more to Him than money. I'm talking about our praise. You say, "Hey, man, I'm good with that. I go to church every Sunday. Sing all those worship songs. Plus, I stream them throughout the week too. So I have the praise thing pretty well covered, thanks."

Some of my more pragmatic readers might be a bit blunter. We make no secret of our self-talk on this issue. "God already knows I love Him. To yak about this all day long doesn't really help anything."

I'm reminded of the man who was asked by a marriage counselor, "Does your wife know that you love her?"

"Of course she does!"

"But how would she know?"

"Look, on our wedding day, I told her I loved her, and if anything ever changed, I promised I'd let her know."

I hope none of us are that stingy—toward a spouse or toward God. Still, what if our fundamental attitude is wrong? What if we *don't* have the "praise thing pretty well covered"? David offers a game-changing challenge in Psalm 70:4, where he says, "May those who love Your salvation say continually, 'May God be exalted!' "

The Hebrew word for *exalted* offers some colorful nuance. It can mean to advance, boast, bring up, exceed, make tall, increase, and magnify. (I'm trying to wrap my brain around the idea of making God taller.) But that's part of what you and I are called to do.

And what about this idea of saying *continually,* "May God be exalted!" Matthew Henry reminds us, "Those that love God's salvation shall say with pleasure, with constant pleasure (for praising God, if we make it our continual work, will be our continual feast), *Let God be magnified,* as he will be, to eternity, in the salvation of his people."[2]

Do you want a continual feast? Do you want to experience continual pleasure even in pain? This is the way. We must learn self-talk that magnifies God all day and all along the way. After all, have you ever seen a truly happy stingy person?

I'd be singing my *own* praises (not to mention lying through my teeth) if I told you I have this all figured out. But here's what I'm finding helpful in my own praise journey.

ACKNOWLEDGE THE BIG THINGS

God picks up His brush and paints a stunning new sky-sized canvas for us 365 days a year. Stop missing those orange-drenched sunrises and sunsets. It's surprisingly easy to stop noticing—and (worse) stop praising. We can't praise what we don't notice. Start noticing big things like sunrises and sunsets. And what about the *crack* of a thunderbolt or the blast of a winter wind? Do we see these as the creative acts of our all-powerful God and give Him the glory?

HOW TO MAKE THIS SELF-TALK YOURS

Look for the Small Things

Don't stop with the obvious—the big and the bold. Find God's glory in the small. Consider the eerie glow of a tiny neon fish, the perfect symmetry of a puffy dandelion, or the silky feel of an infant's back. Praise God for minuscule, everyday beauties. Here's where young children can be our teachers. They excel at this. Everything is worth noticing because everything is new to them—even the small stuff. Notice what *they* notice and give God constant praise.

Lose Your Self-Consciousness

Discipline yourself to praise God for everything you notice that's lovely. Give Him the credit—out loud—right on the spot. As David says in Psalm 34:2, "My soul will make its boast in the LORD; the humble will hear it and rejoice." In other words, your choice to continually exalt God positively affects others. But that won't happen unless "the humble will hear it." Stop being self-conscious. Start being praise-conscious and God-conscious!

On my morning walks, I stroll by a stand of trees that never fails to charge my batteries. I'm learning to say things out loud like, "I love what You've made, God!" or "Everything You make is beautiful." Suddenly, creation becomes a conversation, and God and I are bonding over beauty. Plus, I sometimes share these sightings of God's magnificent work with my wife so "the humble will hear it and rejoice."

God's greatness is so great you can never make too much of it. And because He loves to hear your praise, you'll enjoy giving it to Him.

• • •

SAY IT

"May those who love Your salvation say continually, 'May God be exalted!'"

PSALM 70:4

PRAY IT

Lord,

Forgive me for being stingy.

I have not praised You as I ought.

Worse, I have taken You, Your majesty, and Your creation for granted.

Forgive me, Lord. Take me back to school. Enroll me in Praise 101.

I commit now to doing the homework, longing to give You what You want most.

Help me not to be stingy, Lord.

Not in my giving. Not in my living. Not in my praise.

Amen.

28

FEARING GOD IS A LEARNING PROCESS

Teach me Your way, LORD;
I will walk in Your truth;
unite my heart to fear Your name.

PSALM 86:11

Like most little boys, our son, Tim, was less than thrilled when he was told he would need to go to kindergarten. When he returned from his first day at school, Tim had a smile and a visible sense of relief. In his mind, he'd done it! He'd gone to kindergarten. Check that baby off the list and return to the good life—playing with Hot Wheels all day!

That's when we reminded him that school would be an everyday thing. Gone went the smile. And the next morning, he resisted heading off to kindergarten with the protest, "I already went." Each morning thereafter, he hailed us with a fresh word of resistance, like, "I already learned everything." But our favorite complaint of Tim's was a reference to his teacher: "She talks too much!"

Nevertheless, Tim went. And learned.

Tim's comments remind me of how some of us approach our relationship with God. Some of us get saved but never grow much after that. Like Tim, we feel that "we already went" (prayed the prayer, walked the aisle—whatever). Others of us live our faith in a way that says, "I already learned everything."

But now and then, we bump into reminders, life events, or Bible verses that command us to *fear* God's name. Here, a lot of us are clueless. And who among us hasn't said of the preacher, "He talks too much!"

Part of our problem is ignorance. We hear the word *fear* and say, "No thanks. Don't like fear, so I'm outta here." But the fear that God wants (demands) is a sense of our overwhelming awe of His overwhelming greatness. It's a humility whose first instinct is to kneel and be silent rather than be flippant and familiar. To fear God is to ponder His otherness so regularly and so intently that a rightful trembling of some kind is our inevitable response.

If you look at Scripture, you can't escape the fact that fearing God's name is not merely sort of a big deal to Him. It's *huge*. And we ignore His call at our own peril. But many of us have little interest in fearing God's name, much less learning how to do it.

We engage in self-talk that sounds something like, "Fearing God is a dusty Old Testament concept I don't need in this age of grace." And off we go to play with our Hot Wheels.

But the New Testament is laced with this same command to fear God. In His Luke 18 parable on prayer, Jesus unflatteringly referenced a judge "who did not fear God and did not respect any person" (18:2).

In Romans 3:18, Paul despaired, "There is no fear of God before their eyes."

In 1 Peter 2:17, we're commanded, "Honor all people, love the brotherhood, fear God, honor the king."

In Revelation 14:7, the angel said with a loud voice, "Fear God and give Him glory, because the hour of His judgment has come; worship Him who made the heaven and the earth, and sea and springs of waters."

Can you read those verses and honestly say that fearing God is no longer a big deal? I can't.

Let me suggest better self-talk for this issue: "I need to learn God's way and God's truth. The good news is I *can* learn to fear God." David reached the same conclusion when he wrote in Psalm 86:11, "Teach me Your way, LORD; I will walk in Your truth; unite my heart to fear Your name."

HOW TO MAKE THIS SELF-TALK YOURS

At the risk of making this all seem easy (because it's not), here's the simplified strategy David used: Godly teaching leads to godly walking leads to fearing God.

Let's break this down a bit more.

Godly Teaching

Even a kindergartner knows you're supposed to read the Bible and pray. Is this what David means here? Yes, but maybe in a slightly different way.

Too many of us read our Bibles the way we floss our teeth—too fast and too infrequently to do any good. But you can't go to school once or twice a week for ten minutes and expect to learn much of anything. The same is true with our approach to Bible reading. Nor can you go to church whenever it fits your schedule and expect to be effectively schooled in the fear of God. You can't play hooky or play holy.

God's inspired Word is the exclusive source for the teaching we need. I'm learning it takes an unmovable commitment to unhurried time in the Word of God. And I'm also learning that the more I do this, the more I love the Word.

Godly Walking

David says, "I will walk in Your truth." It's not enough to collect information (and boy, isn't that the problem in so many of our churches?). We were never meant to collect spiritual souvenirs. It's not okay to be taught God's ways and then go on your own. David's statement is a commitment: "I will walk in Your truth."

While traveling to 41 countries, Diana and I brought home enough souvenirs to open a shop featuring international knickknacks and curiosities. Most of them do nothing more than sit on a shelf or collect dust in our attic. By contrast, time spent in the Word is guaranteed to change your walk *away* from godless things and *toward* that which is godly.

Another tool I'm finding helpful is a spiritual journal. For years I resisted it, but the discipline of writing down what God is saying to me through His Word has a way of staying with me and affecting my walk.

One last tool is our choice to invest time with Christlike Christian friends. What a huge resource they can be.

Fearing God

Fearing God is the destination—a lifestyle of listening, learning, and obeying. This is also where unhurried time in prayer is key. How can we truly fear God if we don't know Him? And how can we know Him unless we spend time with Him?

The next time you're hit with a wave of ambivalence about fearing God's name, replace that faulty self-talk with a new commitment to immerse yourself in godly teaching that leads to godly walking that leads to fearing God's name.

• • •

SAY IT

"Teach me Your way, Lord; I will walk in Your truth; unite my heart to fear Your name."

PSALM 86:11

PRAY IT

Lord,

I want to learn to fear Your name. I must learn to fear Your name.

Please teach me Your way.

I want to walk in Your way—I really do!

Would You do whatever heart surgery You need to so that my heart would be united to fear Your name?

I cannot, must not live in any other way.

I ask this all in Jesus' name.

Amen.

29

KNEEL FIRST. KNEEL ALWAYS.

Come, let's worship and bow down,
let's kneel before the Lord our Maker.

PSALM 95:6

A survey from YouGov reveals that 44 percent of Americans never wear a suit, and 45 percent say they wear suits less frequently now than they did ten years ago. Interestingly, 17 percent of Americans merely dislike wearing suits, while another 17 percent hate wearing them.[1]

That survey only underscores that, in America, we don't just sort of like the idea of being casual—we *really* like it! How else can you explain that in addition to casual dress, we have casual dining, casual dating, casual games, casual shoes, casual Fridays, and even casual sex?

Obviously, Americans have cast their ballots, and the landslide winner is...Casual! There's no question that our casual attitude has drizzled over the top of almost every cultural facet.

Libraries—longtime keepers of the quiet—are known today more for their meeting spaces and (noisy) social gatherings. Graduation ceremonies, long rooted in pomp and circumstance, now feel more like the introduction of the starting lineup for a college football team (feel free to cheer). And heaven help the church that doesn't offer a coffee bar—and with it, a warm welcome to sip those beverages during the service. While wearing your jeans. The ones with the holes in the knees. (We're casual.)

I'm not here to condemn coffee and blue jeans at church. I like casual too. In fact, I might just be guilty of *loving* casual. But many of us have swung so far toward the casual that we've fallen for a dangerous deception that has affected our spiritual self-talk. I would argue that many have adopted a mantra that essentially says, "God doesn't care how I worship, so I don't need to concern myself with this."

You've heard that you can worship God in many ways and places, and that's true. But ask David about worship, and he would immediately connect worship with an invitation to kneel and bow—spiritually, if not physically.

I'll never forget a prayer segment at a church meeting where the worship leader went down to his knees and then stretched out and lowered himself even further. And that's how he remained for the next 30 minutes of prayer. His posture had a palpable impact on the entire audience.

At that moment, something inside me said, "This is right! This is good! This is how it should be!" I felt at home, spiritually.

You say, "Well, Jon, just because *you* felt worshipful in that setting doesn't mean it's right for *everyone*." I'm not here to argue. But it's tough, if not foolish, to ignore the Scriptures on this point. The twin concepts of bowing and kneeling before God are found in many places in the Bible.

- " 'It shall be from new moon to new moon and from Sabbath to Sabbath, all mankind will come to bow down before Me,' says the LORD" (Isaiah 66:23).
- "For this reason I bend my knees before the Father" (Ephesians 3:14).

- "At the name of Jesus every knee will bow, of those who are in heaven and on earth and under the earth" (Philippians 2:10).

What about the idea of kneeling before God?

- "He got down on his knees three times a day and prayed and gave thanks before his God, as he had done previously" (Daniel 6:10 ESV).
- "Peter put them all outside, and knelt down and prayed" (Acts 9:40 ESV).

Of course, there are even more dramatic examples of people falling to the ground before the Almighty:

- "All the sons of Israel, seeing the fire come down and the glory of the LORD upon the house, bowed down on the pavement with their faces to the ground" (2 Chronicles 7:3).
- "When He said to them, 'I am He,' they drew back and fell to the ground" (John 18:6).

Indulge me momentarily, and let's explore David's self-talk on this issue. In Psalm 95:6, he says, "Come, let's worship and bow down; let's kneel before the LORD our Maker."

Clearly, this is not a monologue. David is speaking to those around him. To us, even. And what is his grand invitation? To "worship and bow down" and to "kneel before the LORD our Maker." That's certainly not very casual. But doesn't it sound like better self-talk?

Though I have much to learn, I'm a huge fan of bowing down and kneeling in my prayer times. This simple act of obedience blesses me in at least three ways:

1. Kneeling affirms there's Someone more important than my problems.

2. Kneeling reminds me that God is the King—and I'm just a servant.

3. Kneeling makes God bigger and my problems smaller.

There is nothing casual about kneeling before God because there is nothing casual about the Almighty. Why not give it a try? Better yet why not make it a way of life?

HOW TO MAKE THIS SELF-TALK YOURS

Don't wait for a crisis to confront you or a pain to assail you. Start today. Start now.

Why not put this book down, find a private corner, and kneel before God? Spend some unhurried time there. I'm confident you'll experience what David and every other kneeling believer have enjoyed. You'll see that bowing before God...

- refreshes your heart
- enlarges your faith
- shrinks your fears
- quiets your thoughts
- heals your hurts
- anchors your soul

You'll have plenty of time to be casual later today. But right now, it's time to meet your King. Not just any king, but the King of kings. And in His presence, bowing and kneeling are best. Obviously, some of us can't kneel down. Bad knees, limited mobility, or advancing age make the physical act of kneeling or bowing improbable or impossible. But you can still see yourself kneeling before

God in your mind. Ultimately, Scripture says, "The LORD looks at the heart" (1 Samuel 16:7).

The right self-talk: "Whether in my heart or on my knees, I choose a lifestyle of bowing down before God."

• • •

“ SAY IT ”

"Come, let's worship and bow down, let's kneel before the LORD our Maker."

PSALM 95:6

“ PRAY IT ”

Most High God,

You who are the King of kings—

Forgive me for being too familiar, too casual.

Yes, You are my Abba Father, my heavenly Daddy.

But You are also the King who dwells in unapproachable light.

Your Son, Jesus, holds the keys to death and hell.

Therefore, I consider the goodness and severity of God.

I kneel before You. I bow before You.

Teach me to know this as my rightful place in prayer.

Most High God, speak to me as I am low before You.

What do You wish me to know…to confess…to ponder…to do?

I am here. I am listening.

I am Yours.

Amen.

30

I MUST LEARN TO HATE

I will set no worthless thing before my eyes;
I hate the work of those who fall
away; it shall not cling to me.

PSALM 101:3

Every age has its excesses.

In matters of Scripture, each generation struggles with overemphasizing some things while underemphasizing others. We end up with a theological pendulum that swings rather wildly.

Hundreds of years ago, Christians stressed the entirely biblical concept of the severity of God. History has welded the name of Jonathan Edwards to his smoke and sulfur sermon, "Sinners in the Hands of an Angry God." John Bunyan wrote *A Few Sighs from Hell*, a knee-buckling depiction of eternity in the lake of fire. And the legacy of "fire and brimstone" preachers continued all the way into the 1960s.

But then the pendulum slowly swung back toward the (equally biblical) idea that God is love. Today, we've moved so far toward love that we often ignore the fact that God also punishes—and even hates! I see your raised eyebrows, but search the Book for yourself.

Proverbs 6:16-19 explains that God hates "haughty eyes, a lying tongue, and hands that shed innocent blood, a heart that devises wicked plans, feet that run rapidly to evil, a false witness who declares lies, and one who spreads strife among brothers."

Another thing God hates? "The devious are an abomination to the LORD; but He is intimate with the upright" (Proverbs 3:32). And Proverbs 11:1 asserts, "A false balance is an abomination to the LORD, but a just weight is His delight."

These verses are hardly an exhaustive concordance of things God hates, but they indeed establish the fact that...well, God hates. He doesn't *just* love.

More importantly, if we say we want to love God, you and I must also learn to hate—as in hate what God hates. That's a tough sell in our "me 'n' God" buddy culture, but it's as true as any of our favorite verses about the love of God.

Search your soul. Don't you find yourself agitated by all these hate comments? They can be quite unsettling for folks like us whose self-talk often mutters, "God is a God of love—and that's all I need to know or care about."

You and I can mutter that all day, but that doesn't make it true. And worse, that erroneous self-talk can lead to treacherous paths.

The Banias waterfall in northern Israel is reached only by a treacherous path—steep, uneven steps laced with ankle-twisting tree roots. Nonetheless, finally reaching that turquoise ribbon of wetness, hearing its roar, and watching it dancing at the foot of Mount Hermon is nothing short of mesmerizing—and definitely worth the trek.

During one visit, I was determined to capture the perfect photo. I hurried ahead of our group, set up the tripod and camera, and lost all track of time. Eventually, our tour guide, Dr. Charlie Dyer, kindly threaded his way down the path to find me. In the process, he took a major tumble and scraped up his arms and legs. I still feel bad about it.

But you and I lead ourselves and our friends down even more treacherous paths when we entertain self-talk that says, "God is a God of love—and that's all I need to know or care about." It leads to unbiblical thoughts such as, "Sin might not be as sinful as we've been taught." We can even go so far (as many have) to say, "God would never punish people with hell."

But biblical truth is stubborn and unmistakable. If we're going to walk with God, we're going to have to hate what He hates. David shares his self-talk with us in Psalm 101:3, "I will set no worthless thing before my eyes; I hate the work of those who fall away; it shall not cling to me."

You've caught David's strategy here, haven't you? The idea of hating what God hates begins with actively, aggressively removing any "worthless thing" that comes into our lives. Obvious? Maybe. Easy? No.

Your life and mine are drenched and dripping in "worthless things." Charles Spurgeon warns, "What fascinates the eye is very apt to gain admission into the heart."[1]

Whether websites, streaming services, social media, or old-fashioned billboards, we do not lack things that "fascinate the eye." But so many of them are sensual, wicked, and worthless. David's answer? Get rid of them. Or get yourself away from them. Stop hovering. Stop looking. Move on.

Notice that David calls us to "hate the work of those who fall away." In other words, hate the sin but love the sinner.

Most of us know someone who was once on fire for Christ but, for whatever reason, is now stone-cold toward spiritual things. Such a Christless life inevitably leads to words and deeds in which believers should have no part.

We must not engage or entertain a single one of these things. In fact, Spurgeon goes so far as to say, "Hatred of sin is a good sentinel for the door of virtue."[2]

I'll never forget traveling to Israel and visiting the safe rooms of homes that were burned or bombed in the Hamas attack on October 7, 2023. One woman explained that three times, waves of terrorists tried to force open their safe room door. Three times, she and her family fiercely gripped the door handle and warded off death and destruction. But they could never let their guard down. Not for a second. Those who did paid the price.

In the same way, we must never let down our guard against sin and never allow a "worthless thing" before our eyes. The moment we do, there's a price to be paid. But the flip side is that if we run from worthless things and hate the works of those who fall away, we move toward purity and grow more like Christ.

HOW TO MAKE THIS SELF-TALK YOURS

Get Ready!

Worthless things are coming your way—online or in person. Your enemy will see to that. Walk with your eyes open. Expect trouble, not ease. As Paul wrote in Ephesians 6:14, "Stand your ground, putting on the belt of truth and the body armor of God's righteousness" (NLT).

Get Set!

Commit Psalm 101:3 to memory—or carry it in your pocket or purse. This verse is the tool you need at the moment of impact. When that friend who has fallen away says something that chisels away at your faith, or that billboard invites you to set aside your purity, get this verse out. Speak it.

Go!

Be on your way, having wielded the Sword of the Spirit. And walk in confidence, knowing that, as David said of the filth and evil that came across his path, "It shall not cling to me."

If we're going to walk with God, we're going to have to hate what God hates. David helps you talk right, think right, and hate right.

• • •

SAY IT

"I will set no worthless thing before my eyes; I hate the work of those who fall away; it shall not cling to me."

PSALM 101:3

PRAY IT

Father,

Forgive me.

I have not always been vigilant.

You know the worthless things I have set before my eyes—the long parade of things no Christ-follower should look at, let alone follow.

Would You help me live at a different level?

Would You help me embrace biblical self-talk?

Teach me what it means to hate what You hate.

This obedience, *this* lifestyle, *this* holy passion is true love for You.

Amen.

“ 31 ”

LOOK WHERE YOU LOOK

My eyes shall be upon the faithful of the land,
that they may dwell with me.

PSALM 101:6

Conning the crowd.

That's what my brothers and I did as our family and a hundred others gathered to watch the eruption of "Old Faithful," Yellowstone's most iconic treasure. This thermal geyser erupts with such regularity that signs are posted so tourists can gather to see the blast—which typically shoots water nearly 150 feet into the air. Definitely worth seeing.

The thing is, the posted eruption time is "fairly close"—but definitely not precise. When our family visited, it was before the age of smartphones and digital cameras. If you wanted a picture, you needed a real camera with actual film. And back then, a roll of film maxed out at 36 shots, so you couldn't just mash your finger over the shutter as often as you wanted and somehow delete the bad shots. No, a definite sense of stewardship and restraint was required.

My mischievous brothers and I circulated throughout the crowd, our cameras at the ready. And at the slightest sign of water coming from the base of Old Faithful, we would cry, "There it is!" At the same time, we would fake like we were taking a photo. At least a dozen other cameras clicked off wasted shots. We would wait a few minutes, and at the next false start, we would repeat our urgent claim, "There it is!" And then—click, click, click—20 more people suckered for another dud shot. (Looking back, it's clear my immature prank was wrong—and selfish. Fun at someone else's expense is never Christlike.)

Eventually, the geyser finally erupted, but not before a lot of people wasted a whole lot of film. Yet apparently even Old Faithful isn't so faithful. According to scientists, the time between eruptions has steadily increased over the last 30 years. Maybe they should rename the thing "Old Not-as-Faithful."

Pardon the hairpin turn as I ask, Where are you at regarding biblical faithfulness? Are you growing in faithfulness? Or, with the passage of time, are you becoming "Old Not-as Faithful"?

Throughout Scripture, God places a high premium on faithfulness. In Christ's famous parable of the talents, we read this commendation of the faithful servants: "You were faithful with a few things, I will put you in charge of many things; enter the joy of your master" (Matthew 25:21).

In Luke 16:10, Jesus declares, "The one who is faithful in a very little thing is also faithful in much; and the one who is unrighteous in a very little thing is also unrighteous in much."

Faithfulness is one of the fruits of the Spirit listed in Galatians 5:22. And in 1 Corinthians 4:2, we're told, "Moreover, it is required of stewards that they be found faithful" (ESV).

Anyone who's gone through troubles and testing knows firsthand that faithfulness comes at a high price. Yet, ironically, we are often quick to devalue or minimize the extraordinarily expensive trait known as faithfulness. Our self-talk can degenerate so far that we can actually believe nonsense such as, "Faithfulness isn't all that big a deal. I can show up at church on Sundays and live the rest of my life my way."

In other words, we come to believe that faithfulness is essential some of the time. Why is this such a big deal? Because it leads to big-time foolishness. We can move toward a lifestyle of honoring Christ on Sundays but living for ourselves the rest of the week. Do that long enough, and you end up at the gates of eternity with nothing more than a lukewarm faith and a lifetime of blown opportunities.

David offers us better self-talk when he draws a line in the sand in Psalm 101:6. He testifies, "My eyes shall be upon the faithful of the land, that they may dwell with me." Note—just as in David's day, there are plenty of unfaithful people in our land, plenty of ungodly people around. But David says, "My eyes shall be upon the faithful." In other words, you and I can learn to look at the ways of the godly constantly—and imitate them! Note further that this is a choice—a *daily* choice. However, there are two huge benefits to this better self-talk.

BENEFIT #1: STAYING FOCUSED ON GODLY PEOPLE KEEPS OUR OWN FOCUS ON GODLY THINGS

We become like those we are with, right? When we travel internationally, my wife has observed that it takes very little time for me to pick up the accent of whatever host I'm with. However they pronounce words, I start pronouncing them the same without even thinking about it.

In much the same way, we speak the same accent of faithfulness that our closest friends have. Their love for Christ (or lack of love) rubs off on us. That's why we must choose godly and faithful friends.

BENEFIT #2: DWELLING WITH THE FAITHFUL KEEPS US FROM THE UNFAITHFUL

David's desire for faithful people is "that they may dwell with me." We can't just be with them occasionally. We must dwell with them constantly by doing life with them.

These should be the people we text, email, dine with, and pray with the most. The best defense against unfaithfulness is to live with faithful people. There needs to be more than just hanging out once in a while. Over time, you can learn to constantly look at the ways of the godly and imitate them.

HOW TO MAKE THIS SELF-TALK YOURS

Ask yourself, *Do I honestly value faithfulness the way God does?* It begins with the choice to care about what God cares about. Faithfulness in little things is a big thing.

Have you made the deliberate choice that the spiritually faithful will be your closest friends? Maybe you need to spend less time with some *less* faithful friends. Perhaps you need to pursue more godly, more faithful friends.

One other sobering thought. A person who is faithful in every situation is simply called faithful. There is no "105 percent faithful." There's no such thing as "extra faithful." And when you think about it, "mostly faithful" is an oxymoron. In marriage, you're either faithful to your spouse or you're not. The same is true with your relationship with God. When our family visited Old Faithful, my brothers and I may have conned the crowd, but there is no conning God. He knows everything—including whether or not you are faithful.

The next time you're tempted to believe that faithfulness isn't all that big a deal, pull out this verse. Let it draw you to a fresh commitment to the Lord. But remember—you're not in this struggle by yourself. First Thessalonians 5:24 assures us, "Faithful is He who calls you, and He also will do it." We can and must live a life of godly faithfulness. When we do, we invite God's notice and are completely at home with Him.

• • •

SAY IT

"My eyes shall be upon the faithful of the land, that they may dwell with me."

PSALM 101:6

PRAY IT

Father,

I want to be faithful. Your Son was faithful. I must be faithful.

Help me to know whom I should spend less time with. Whisper their names to me, Lord. But whisper loudly, lest I fail to hear. And having heard, grant me the courage to transition lovingly to others who are more faithful to You.

Like David, I want my eyes to be on the faithful, that they may dwell with me.

Thank You for Your promise, "Faithful is He who calls you, and He also will do it."

Amen.

32

WATCH WHERE YOU WALK

One who walks in a blameless way
is one who will serve me.

PSALM 101:6

Confession: I love watching the different ways people walk. Because our kitchen faces the street, while eating dinner, we often see people going for strolls. The different cadences and walking styles are fascinating.

One lady takes this strange dip at every step as if she's starting to go downstairs and then comes back up. And we've noticed her kids all do the same thing. There's another guy who appears to stumble more than walk as he strolls down the street. Two school buddies make their daily trek to the school bus, but their heads are always down, peering at their phones. My wife's favorite is a lady whose dog is always clenching a stick in his mouth. Then there are the "I'm totally serious" folks who flail their arms purposefully for full cardiac benefit. These people all tend to scowl. Is it because the arm thing is so strenuous, or are they just trying to impress the rest of us that they're really doing the work?

Because my feet point outward, a friend, Bill, has labeled my penguin-like strides as "Y-walking." Ask my grandkids, and they will be happy to perform their best impression of that walk.

But, as we turn a corner here, I ask, What about our *spiritual* walk? What exactly does that look like—particularly from heaven's perspective?

It turns out that how we walk before God is of enormous interest to the Almighty—and it should also be to us. In fact, how someone walks in daily life inevitably offers make-or-break clues as to whether or not we should hang out with them.

Of course, few of us might be so arrogant as to say, "My walk with God is just fine, thank you."

Once, while driving on the expressway, we passed a 53-foot semitrailer that was nondescript at best. But the name on the cab door of the hauling company arrested my attention: "Beyond Reproach."

Rolling down the highway of life, is that what your life looks like, "Beyond Reproach"? More often than not, the cab hauling my life might more honestly be labeled "Beyond Confused" or "Beyond Belief." (As in, "I can't believe that a Christian like me could think/say/do something like that.")

In truth, when it comes to this business of walking blamelessly before God, there is no end to the negative self-talk that forces its way into our thinking. During darker moments, we tell ourselves things like, "I'm not sure I'll ever get my act together enough to serve God meaningfully. I guess it's beyond me."

David's self-talk in Psalm 101:6 reminds us of just how critical "right walking" is. He says, "One who walks in a blameless way is one who will serve me." In other words, "All you folks with a questionable walk, don't bother applying. There's no room for you." That's how crucial proper walking was to David. And it must be to us.

But here's the really good news: We can change. We can grow. We can walk better. And that's the self-talk we need to engage in. We need to tell ourselves, "I *can* learn to walk in a blameless way. Then God can truly use me to serve Him."

If this were not possible, David would not and could not have written, "One who walks in a blameless way is one who will serve me." He wouldn't be so cavalier as to toss out an impossible standard, a goal we could never achieve.

My point is that it *is* realistic. It's doable! But this doesn't happen automatically, that's for sure. So how can we make this personal? How do we make this biblical self-talk *our* self-talk?

BLAMELESS WALKING TAKES FORETHOUGHT

I love to plan trips, especially international trips. It's fun to book the most reasonable flights, find the best hotel values, and research the best sites to see. Traveling internationally by yourself can be tricky, so you really must give all this a lot of forethought. If you're not careful, you might book a hotel that's a 90-minute cab ride from the airport.

Traveling through life in a God-honoring way takes no less planning and forethought.

The old business maxim is also true for our spiritual business: If you aim at nothing, you'll hit it every time. Decide today that you want to walk in a blameless way before God. Tell Him you want that. He'll love hearing it from your lips. And He'll be the first to cheer you on.

HOW TO MAKE THIS SELF-TALK YOURS

As believers, many of us have the mistaken idea that godliness—or, in this case, learning to walk in a blameless way—should somehow *happen* to us. Nope. *You* have to do the walking. And that takes effort.

Have you heard about the GPS for seniors? It not only tells you how to get where you're going—but also *why* you want to get there. But as you chuckle, consider that when it comes to walking in a blameless way, it isn't just seniors who struggle with remembering why we want to get there. Thankfully, David reminds us that the one living in a blameless way is the one God can and will use.

Get ready to expend some effort. And don't beat yourself up when you make a wrong turn. Get back on the path with the assurance that you'll be blessed at every step and are ready to serve God. More than that, an unfailing Guide will be with you as you attempt to walk in a blameless way.

• • •

SAY IT

"One who walks in a blameless way
is one who will serve me."

PSALM 101:6

PRAY IT

Great Shepherd of the sheep—

You know my tendency to wander.

To leave the right path.

To know what is right—and not do it.

I confess this spirit of waywardness. I repent of my wrong-way attitude.

Lord, would You help me to walk in a blameless way? I want to be used of You.

So whisper at every turn. Shout when You need to shout. Keep me in step with the Spirit.

I humbly ask You.

In Christ's name.

Amen.

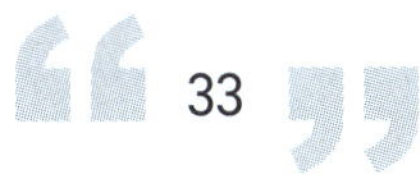

YOUR SINS ARE GONE—TOTALLY GONE

As far as the east is from the west,
so far has He removed our wrongdoings from us.

PSALM 103:12

When hiking through the desert of Tatooine, stay well clear of the Great Pit of Carkoon. Here dwells the sarlaac, a mythical multitentacled creature known for its gaping mouth. According to Star Wars lore, the sarlaac digests its victims for a thousand years.

In the Star Wars franchise, there seems to be no end to creepy characters—fictional but frightening. Oddly, you and I have a remarkable capacity for creating our own hideous behemoths. They look and sound as real as anything George Lucas ever splashed on the big screen.

Consider the brute known as Self-Condemnation. Unlike the sarlaac, which is (fortunately) confined to the Great Pit of Carkoon, Self-Condemnation can dig a hole into almost any heart any place at any time.

Little else is as welcoming to the larvae of Self-Condemnation as a heart that reads Scripture but does not truly believe it. You say, "That's not me, Jon. I believe every word of Scripture is inspired and true." That's great. But your belief is more than your words.

Forgiveness—or, more specifically, the lack of feeling forgiven—has become a monster of epic proportions for too many of us. We read verses like 1 John 1:9—"If we confess our sins, He is faithful and righteous, so that He will forgive us our sins and cleanse us from all unrighteousness"—and even happily quote them, but down deep, we do not believe.

That secret skepticism comes at a price. Every failure to believe God's Word on being forgiven signals a feeding time for the monster of Self-Condemnation. We doubt. It grows. We doubt more. It grows bigger.

Before long we embrace a wicked message in our self-talk: "The guilt from my past sins never stops eating at me. I guess I'm doomed to a life of self-condemnation." Worst of all, we learn to live like this, eaten away every day—one self-condemning thought at a time. At some point, we must honestly ask, "Is this existence much different than the fate of being swallowed by a sarlaac?"

Though somewhere in our heart we know the Word of God is true, we can't seem to make it true for *us*. Others, maybe. But not us. Why can we read in our Bibles that our sins are forgiven but fail to live that way?

For questions like those, we need to consider the perspective of the man we know as David. How did he address this problem? After all, with murder and adultery in his past, he surely must have wrestled with occasional thoughts of self-condemnation. What did he learn that can help us with our broken self-talk?

In Psalm 103:12, we encounter David's self-talk on this forgiveness issue. His language is so wildly hopeful that it strikes us as hyperbole. Only it's not. David says, "As far as the east is from the west, so far has He removed our wrongdoings from us."

Imagine that NASA has built two rockets designed to be easy enough for civilians to fly. They have asked you and one of your friends to command one rocket each during a first-ever simultaneous launch. Blasting upward at 25,000 miles an hour, you escape Earth's gravity. At the same time, your friend turns on a booster that sets him on an easterly course while your instructions are to head due west.

Sorry for reminding you of fifth-grade math, but stay with me here. Traveling at 25,000 miles per hour, you would be separated by 50,000 miles after one hour! In just 24 hours, the gap would be 1,200,000 miles (earning enough frequent flier points to take your extended family to Hawaii). Assuming you had unlimited fuel and could travel an unlimited distance, you would get sick and tired of freeze-dried space food, but you wouldn't be even one inch closer to the point where east meets west.

Here me clearly—this verse is not merely a mathematical theory. It is literally true. God's astounding claim that He has removed our sins as far as the east is from the west is something we should regularly get lost in. As Charles Spurgeon observes, "If sin be removed so far, then we may be sure that the scent, the trace, the very memory of it must be entirely gone."[1]

It's time to replace our wrong self-talk with the right self-talk. Try this on for size: "I can live free from the guilt of my sins as I cling to God's promise that He has personally removed them."

I absolutely love and need this better self-talk. Maybe you do too? Are you wired for guilt? For whatever reason, some of us seem to be. There's false guilt, actual guilt, and past guilt. Sadly, we're not choosy. If guilt is there, we reach for it.

But this passage, this biblical self-talk, is so freeing! And it's not a one-off. David doesn't speak in a spiritual vacuum. Check out these verses:

- "I, I alone, am the one who wipes out your wrongdoings for My own sake, and I will not remember your sins" (Isaiah 43:25).

- "There is now no condemnation at all for those who are in Christ Jesus" (Romans 8:1).
- "Forgive as the Lord forgave you" (note the past tense!) (Colossians 3:13 NIV).
- "If we confess our sins, He is faithful and righteous, so that He will forgive us our sins and cleanse us from all unrighteousness" (1 John 1:9).

HOW TO MAKE THIS SELF-TALK YOURS

First—a reality check. If you've been suffering from false guilt and repeated accusations, you've probably established some deep-rutted wrong thought patterns. Thinking biblically will replace those old patterns, but it will take time. Don't be discouraged!

More than time, you'll also need discipline—and lots of it. The next time—and every time—the evil creature of self-condemnation eats at your innards, grab this verse. Say it loud! And say it again. I promise you, over time, you can starve that monster as you feed your soul the life-giving truth of God's Word.

• • •

SAY IT

"As far as the east is from the west, so far has He removed our wrongdoings from us."

PSALM 103:12

PRAY IT

Great God of all forgiveness—

Thank You!

Thank You that Your Word is true.

Thank You that with You, not only is forgiveness possible, but so is freedom from self-condemnation.

Lord, I have much work to do here. Please guide me.

Would You help me starve self-condemnation and feed on Your promise instead?

I long to replace my negative self-talk with Your very own words.

In faith, I anticipate that the peace of God, which surpasses all comprehension, will guard my heart and mind through Christ Jesus (Philippians 4:7).

Amen.

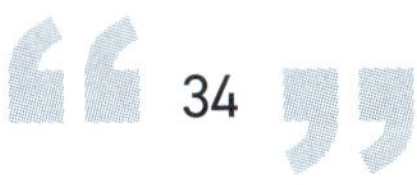

HE GETS YOU

He Himself knows our form;
He is mindful that we are nothing but dust.

PSALM 103:14

As a toddler, my cousin overheard his grandmother describing something she'd goofed up rather badly. Entering the conversation, the little guy offered this sympathetic reassurance: "That's okay, Grandma. We all make steaks."

You may have already noticed that the quickest way to get attention is to make a mistake. The problem is that the only thing most people learn from their gaffes is how to blame *other* people for them.

But while most of us excel at blaming others, we are also oddly committed to labeling, cataloging, and reviewing our own many blunders. We file them away in readily accessible mental cabinets—which is bad enough. The real trouble comes when we yank open those cabinets and dig for memories of messes we've made.

I won't pretend to speak for you, but I'm guessing you have a sufficient stash of flubs, faults, and faux pas to keep you red-faced every day until the end of the century.

The real problem is not that we have mistakes in our past but that we drag them into our present. This leads us into damaging self-talk that grumbles self-accusations such as, "I mess up so much and so often, I'm sure God is tired of me—real tired." I've said this very thing many times.

But that is a lie—and a lousy one at that. I know this because I overheard David's self-talk in Psalm 103.

Almost universally, Bible scholars agree that this psalm was written later in David's life. Who cares about that? You and I do. Because his words have added weight at this point. By now, David had made many more messes than when he was younger. His failures now bulged the walls of the mental cabinets of his memory—meaning many available options for review.

David could have fallen for the self-talk many of us gravitate toward: "I've messed up too much. I'm sure God can hardly stand to be around me." But David knew that thinking to be ridiculous. What was his perspective, then?

In Psalm 103:14, as David pondered the God he loved but failed—the God *you* love but have failed—he declared, "He Himself knows our form; He is mindful that we are nothing but dust."

There's something freeing about admitting our limitations, right? But how incredible to think that despite our foibles and fallenness, God is kind enough to be mindful without being vengeful. Three simple truths jump out at us from this verse.

1. GOD REMEMBERS THAT YOU ARE DUST

The Hebrew word for *remember*, used here, means to call to mind. In other words, God's understanding of your limitations is something He regularly reminds Himself of. It's not a stashed-way, far-away factoid. In His infinite patience and grace, your dustiness is something He takes into account. He's like the dad forever reminding himself that two-year-olds have limitations.

2. *YOU* SHOULD REMEMBER THAT YOU ARE DUST

If God remembers that you are dust, shouldn't you? I don't toss this out as some blanket coverage for our bad behavior. God offers no such thing. Still, many of us quickly beat ourselves up over a lack of progress, overcoming a besetting sin or a bad habit. At some point in the struggle, there's a place for pausing and remembering that you are just dust. That's what this verse is for. Here is the very self-talk we need.

3. DUSTY PEOPLE NEED A SPOTLESS SAVIOR

In John 15:5, Jesus declared, "Apart from Me you can do nothing." That makes total sense when we finally believe that we are "nothing but dust." We need Jesus! First Peter 1:19 describes Jesus as a "lamb unblemished and spotless." And if you are following Christ, Ephesians 5:27 assures you that God wants to present you to Himself, "having no spot or wrinkle or any such thing...holy and blameless." But if we're going to attain this goal, we need the spotless Savior, Jesus.

Could I gently ask you if you've acknowledged your need for Jesus? It begins with asking Him to forgive your wrongdoing, your sins. Then ask Him to help you turn away from this garbage. Invite Jesus to be in charge of all that you are. The Bible word is Savior. Jesus was and is spotless. And we all need that spotless Savior.

HOW TO MAKE THIS SELF-TALK YOURS

1. Thank God that He knows your limitations. Thank Him for His grace and patience with you.
2. Thank God that He knows your mistakes. The Hebrew word for "knows," *yada*, means God knows us relationally, personally, and deeply, not just intellectually. Not to point out the obvious, but He has full knowledge of

every mistake you've ever made—or will make—and loves you anyway.

3. Ask for His help in releasing the memories of your messes to Him. It's time to end all that midnight (or midday) tiptoeing up and down the hallways of your mind. It's time to leave those mental file cabinets alone—forever. Only God can help us win here, so ask for that help!

• • •

SAY IT

"He Himself knows our form; He is mindful that we are nothing but dust."

PSALM 103:14

PRAY IT

Heavenly Father—

I cannot fully understand this.

You know my mind, my bent (and how bent that mind can be), but You love me anyway.

Thank You for knowing me intimately but also being infinitely patient.

Thank You for being mindful that I am but dust.

Could You help me to remember this too?

Help me learn to replace my negative self-talk with this amazing claim.

Lord, help me strike a biblical balance between pushing toward growth and holiness while acknowledging my dustiness.

In Christ's spotless name.

Amen.

35

YOUR ENEMIES ARE GOD'S PROBLEM

Through God we will do valiantly,
and it is He who will trample down our enemies.

PSALM 108:13

You have enemies. You will have enemies until the day you die.

On that cheery note, shall we grab a bite of lunch?

Truth be told, it's time we came to grips with the inevitability of enemies. A pastor once preached a sermon on the importance of forgiving our enemies. About 15 minutes into his message, he wanted to gauge his congregation's reaction. He asked them to raise their hands if they were now willing to forgive their enemies. About half did so. At the conclusion of this powerfully convicting sermon, he polled the people again. This time, only one elderly lady refused to raise her hand.

After the church service, the pastor asked her why she didn't feel the need to forgive. After all, with nearly a century of living, she was bound to have plenty of enemies.

"Nope," she calmly countered. "I don't have enemies. I outlived 'em all! Every last rotten snake in the bunch!" So...what about the rest of us who *haven't* outlived our enemies?

Your enemy might be a coworker or even a boss. It feels as though they have had it out for you from day one. You're constantly looking over your shoulder because you feel as if your job is on the line.

Your enemy might be a neighbor. My wife and I know a couple whose neighbor down the street claims to know Christ, but his actions and words are aggressively hurtful and angry.

Your enemy might be a jealous sibling. The division started in childhood, and whatever the problem was, it was never ironed out. Over time, the sense of enmity became palpable. At holiday gatherings, it feels as though there's a demilitarized zone between you—and nobody dares cross over.

Your enemy might be an addiction, a fear, or a failure you can't get past. Your enemy might be loneliness or selfishness or cancer or a financial hole so deep you feel you'll be sucked in, never to be heard from again.

One of my enemies is the fear of messing up while speaking. In a recurring dream, I have a white-knuckle grip on a pulpit while I'm blathering nonsensically, having forgotten my notes at home.

Of course, all of us have fears much more intense than this. But how do we cope with the ongoing presence of these fears, let alone fight against them? And what are we to make of the enemies we can't even see?

Paul tells us in Ephesians 6:12, "Our struggle is not against flesh and blood, but against the rulers, against the powers, against the world forces of this darkness, against the spiritual forces of wickedness in the heavenly places." All of which means you have enemies—those you can see and those you can't.

All of this talk about enemies is not exactly a dose of melatonin to troubled souls like ours. Is it any wonder that so many of us engage in wrong self-talk? We tell our souls, "My adversaries are too many and too great. Why pretend to put up a fight?"

Thankfully, for outgunned, outnumbered folks like us, David

offers more helpful self-talk in Psalm 108:13. He reminds himself, "Through God we will do valiantly, and it is He who will trample down our enemies."

That's a lot different than the mournful tune most of us naysayers sing. And you have to love David's certainty: "Through God we *will* do valiantly." But being a good Bible student, you've already picked up on the importance of that first phrase, "Through God."

When it came to fighting flesh and blood enemies, David was no theorist. Remember, he'd cut off Goliath's head. In combat across the country, he'd used his sword, sling, bow, and shield—not to mention his bare hands! With all of that in the rearview mirror, David confidently sums up, "Through God we will do valiantly, and it is He who will trample down our enemies."

HOW TO MAKE THIS SELF-TALK YOURS

It's a great promise, and we love David's confidence. But how do we make his self-talk ours? Your enemies are a problem. The only question is, Will you let them be *God's* problem or yours? Seems to me that what we need is a "Triple-A Strategy." Consider these three steps for wimpier warriors like us.

Acknowledge your enemies. David did. His many psalms are heavy with the stench of bad guys. Ironically, acknowledging our fears brings a strange freedom. Conversely, there's a heaviness that comes from pretending they don't exist. David has no problem naming them, and neither should you.

Admonish your fears. It's not enough to identify them. We must remind ourselves that God is greater than our fears. All of them. We do that by (no surprise at this point in the book!) speaking the words of this verse. That phrase, "Through God we will do valiantly," is a terrific way to verbally admonish your fears. Claim it as your battle cry.

Anticipate God's win. David's self-talk includes the confident conclusion, "It is He who will trample down our enemies." David doesn't say God "could" or "might." He speaks, thinks, and acts as though God's victory is a done deal already. And it is. Just remember whom to thank, praise, and magnify on the other side of the conflict.

• • •

SAY IT

"Through God we will do valiantly, and it is He who will trample down our enemies."

PSALM 108:13

PRAY IT

Mighty God—

You rule over nations and kingdoms and conflicts.

I love this promise of doing valiantly through You.

Up until now, I have been anything but valiant.

But I stand alongside David, knowing I am promised a valiant victory through You.

Mighty God, would You trample down every wicked enemy in my path?

Would You do this in such a way that I am forever enamored of Your awesome deliverance?

Thank You that I do not have to fear any enemy.

Instead, I choose to adore You, great King of all kings.

Amen.

NO EXPIRATION DATE

The L*ORD will accomplish what concerns me;*
Your faithfulness, L*ORD, is everlasting;*
do not abandon the works of Your hands.

PSALM 138:8

It started back in the 1970s when America began waking up to the fact that we were a nation of overweight, underexercised heart attacks waiting to happen. People traded in bowling shoes for jogging shoes. And we took a long, hard look at the high-salt, high-fat, high-cholesterol diets we had previously accepted as normal.

In the wake of this awakening, there was a similar concern about the condition of our nation's food supply. Could we really trust the contents of the cans and boxes in our grocery store? Didn't we deserve to know how long we could store these items before they lost nutritional value—or worse, could harm us?

That's when "Best Used By" stickers made their grand appearance. Since then, expiration dates have become a huge (if not confusing) staple in today's grocery business. We want to know how long our milk, mayonnaise, or mashed potatoes will last.

Recently, I found a small stash of single-serve apple sauce cups in my office. I noted that they were two years out of date. But at this point, the situation was a borderline science experiment, and I just had to know how bad that applesauce really was. I peeled off the aluminum lid expecting to see green fuzz—or worse. But there was no hint of mold, and it even smelled right. I gave that apple sauce a tentative taste, and then I ate the whole cup without incident. It's enough to make you question those expiration dates.

Similarly, many of us question whether God's promises come with an expiration date. Though we would never say so publicly, we wonder—and we're nervous. We're painfully aware that we mess up—lots. This leads many of us into a conversation with ourselves where we whisper accusingly, "Because I don't always obey God, I can't always expect His favor."

But is that true? Is that even biblical? Is that the kind of self-talk a Christ-follower should engage in?

Like all of us, David probably wrestled with these same issues. He lets us in on his self-talk in Psalm 138:8, "The Lord will accomplish what concerns me; Your faithfulness, Lord, is everlasting; do not abandon the works of Your hands."

Two truths fairly shout at us in this passage from the shepherd king. And both of those truths are mighty reassuring.

First, note that the Lord does the accomplishing. David stresses that "the Lord will accomplish what concerns me." It's not on you. It's not on your strength or smarts or performance. The Lord does the accomplishing.

Second, note that *the Lord's* faithfulness matters most. Your obedience matters, and your faithfulness matters. But God's faithfulness is everlasting. It always lasts.

Does this mean we can do as we please? No. More specifically, does this mean we can sin and not expect consequences? No. Though God forgives us, He does not remove us from the damage created by our choices. An old saying reminds us that while we do get to choose our sins, we don't get to choose our consequences. No sin ever came with a magic wand for erasing its damage. Indeed, the only "magic" attached to sin is its dark power to convince us we can somehow get away with it.

HOW TO MAKE THIS SELF-TALK YOURS

When our daughter, Lynnette, was learning to talk, her version of the word *remind* came out as "me-mind." But that says it better than the original. In the same spirit, here are three "me-minders" to hang on to as we attempt to change our self-talk

Me-Minder #1: God Will Not Abandon Me

Hebrews 13:5 assures us, "He Himself has said, 'I will never desert you, nor will I ever abandon you.' " God must really want us to get this because the writer of Hebrews is restating a promise God made to Joshua: "No one will be able to oppose you all the days of your life. Just as I have been with Moses, I will be with you; I will not desert you nor abandon you" (Joshua 1:5). The bottom line is that God isn't going anywhere, regardless of how much you or I mess up.

Me-Minder #2: My Acceptance Is Not Based on My Performance

One of the enemy's most hideous lies is that God's acceptance of us is entirely wrapped up in how well we do at obeying and serving Him. When we do well, He accepts us, according to this lie. And conversely, when we mess up, we are rejected. But in John 6:37, Jesus promised, "The one who comes to Me I certainly will not cast out." Listen to the powerful imagery of Isaiah 49:15-16, where God asks, "Can a woman forget her nursing child and have no compassion on the son of her womb? Even these may forget, but I will not forget you. Behold, I have inscribed you on the palms of My hands; your walls are continually before Me." You do not have to earn God's favor or acceptance. You already have all that He has to give. Tell yourself to stop performing and start enjoying God's full acceptance because of Christ.

Me-Minder #3: God Is Faithful Even When I Am Not

You and I are going to fail. We're going to be unfaithful. But even in the face of that, God remains faithful. Here's the proof in 2 Timothy 2:13, where Paul assures us, "If we are faithless, He remains faithful, for He cannot deny Himself." Further, we're counseled in Hebrews 10:23 to "hold firmly to the confession of our hope without wavering, for He who promised is faithful." Does the Holy Spirit grieve when we are unfaithful? Yes. But does He turn away from us in like unfaithfulness? Absolutely not. That's worth recalling.

• • •

SAY IT

"The LORD will accomplish what concerns me; Your faithfulness, LORD, is everlasting; do not abandon the works of Your hands."

PSALM 138:8

PRAY IT

Heavenly Father—

I am amazed at Your eternal faithfulness.

Unshakable. Inexhaustible. Unfathomable.

Thank You for this pearl of great price—Your unwavering, unending faithfulness. Yet merely offering thanks seems small and cheap for so great a grace.

Receive not just my thanks but my prayer for daily faithfulness in my walk with You.

I thank You and praise You for this better self talk from David.

Amen.

37

VOICE YOUR FEARS

I cry out with my voice to the Lord;
with my voice I implore the Lord for compassion.

PSALM 142:1

Caves. They are neither comfortable nor comforting. As everyone knows, they are filled with creepy things like bats, spiders, snakes, and scorpions. Observe that no cave is home to a Starbucks or McDonald's. In all the years of wild and crazy reality TV, no one has yet to produce a single episode of *Extreme Cave Makeover*. A public figure no less notable than the Geico caveman doesn't even dwell in a cave! And come to think of it, neither did the Flintstones.

Though people have lived in caves for thousands of years, caves are not good for sleeping (too hard) or cooking (too smoky). As for keeping you dry, most caves drip with condensation or other moisture—not good!

But in David's story, a surprising number of chapters unfolded inside a cave. That's true of Psalm 142. On the run from King Saul, David was once again holed up in a cave. Was it Adullam? En Gedi? We're not told. And in one sense, it doesn't matter (a cave is a cave).

Just know that David was in a dark, dank place. And his fears were much worse than the bite from a snake or the sting of a scorpion. A wealthy and powerful foe with virtually unlimited manpower and resources was determined to track David down, drag him out, and end his life.

What David needed then was not an extreme cave makeover but an extreme *heart* makeover. He knew it was the only way he could survive the pressure. What did David do?

I'll answer that question very specifically after we talk—very specifically—about *you*. Are you a cave dweller? I'm serious. In a physical sense, you might recline on a couch and sleep in a bed—but emotionally, your world feels as hard as rock.

Traveling to Israel's oasis of En Gedi near Masada, you see not one or two caves but dozens of them. Maybe hundreds? The point is, there was no shortage of places for David to hole up and hide out. Though we live thousands of miles away, the same is true for us today—so many caves!

- You might live in a cave of concern for a marriage that's grown as cold as stone.
- You might live in a cave of cluelessness over a prodigal son or daughter who is tearing your family apart.
- You might live in a cave of condemnation over the depression you can't seem to shake but fear to admit to others.
- You might live in a cave of cowardliness, knowing you need to take a godly stand but fearing repercussions from your boss, family, or friends.
- You might live in a cave of catastrophe, having suffered the death of a child, sibling, or spouse.

- You might live in a cave of captivity, held fast by memories of abuse or neglect.
- You might live in a cave of crippling concern over the likely loss of your job, home, or reputation. You're a pastor who needs pastoring or a caretaker who can no longer take care—and you're anguished.

While living in a cave—any cave—it's easy to engage in damaging self-talk. Alarmingly, we can get to the place where thoroughly grounded, church-attending, Bible-reading folks like us convince ourselves, "Telling God about my fears doesn't help." Obviously, we would never say that to our kids, but practically, that's how we live (and by the way—we're not fooling our kids, either).

But David learned to use better self-talk. His message is one you and I can leverage today. Listen to how David encouraged himself in Psalm 142:1. He says, "I cry out with my voice to the Lord; with my voice I implore the Lord for compassion."

HOW TO MAKE THIS SELF-TALK YOURS

For all of us cave-dwellers, David says it's time to have a laser-focused conversation with God. That conversation should include two components. Let's call them *Cave Busters* because, if prayed in the right spirit, that's exactly what they are.

Cave Buster #1: "I cry out with my voice to the Lord."

When was the last time you did this? You say, "Gimme a break! I pray about my struggle every single day!" Fine. But when did you last "cry out" as David did? Loudly! Intensely! The Bible does not suggest that when you reach the right threshold of emotionalism, your problems will all be solved, but we are encouraged not merely to *mention* our need but to cry out. Start there.

Cave Buster #2: "I implore the Lord for compassion."

Isn't it interesting that David implores the Lord not for a military triumph over Saul (his implacable foe and the reason David is in a cave)? Instead, David implores the Lord for His compassion, something way bigger and better. Haven't you noticed? God's pockets are not merely full but *bulging* with compassion. That's because He bakes a new batch every day. Lamentations 3:23 assures us His compassion and mercy are "new every morning."

List your cares. Cry out to God—loudly. Ask for His compassion. And don't forget to thank Him as He takes you by the hand and walks you right out of your cave.

• • •

SAY IT

"I cry out with my voice to the LORD; with my voice I implore the LORD for compassion."

PSALM 142:1

PRAY IT

Heavenly Father,

I am weary of doing life in a cave.

I am weary of feeling like, talking like, living like there is no hope or help.

Father, I read David's words. His self-talk.

I want a way out of my cave. You have invited me to cry out.

More than that, You have invited me to implore You for compassion.

So here I am, Lord. As best I can, with all I am, hear me now.

Knowing You're listening, I cry out for ______________.

I implore You for compassion regarding ______________.

Thank You for hearing, for caring, for answering.

Thank You that I don't have to stay in my cave any longer.

In Christ's freeing name.

Amen.

38

GIVE HIM YOUR COMPLAINTS

I pour out my complaint before Him;
I declare my trouble before Him.

PSALM 142:2

I bet you've seen the meme about the company complaint form. It's an 8.5 x 11-inch sheet of paper that features a minuscule box half the size of a postage stamp. The caption reads, "Enter complaint here" (meaning inside that teensy box).

On the flip side, there are folks who seem to love to complain—almost *live* to complain. The way some people find fault, you would think there's a reward! These folks go through life standing at the complaint counter wearing the same thing every single day: a scowl. Honestly, if faultfinding tapped into the electrical grid, some people would be a powerhouse!

If you have ever held a job in the public service sector, you'll understand one frustrated worker who quipped, "I now understand my fascination with goldfish. Their mouths are always open but never complaining."

While it's easy to grumble, my experience is that many Christ-followers are reluctant to initiate a serious concern or dissent with

Deity. As decent, polite folks who genuinely love Christ, we hold back from sharing our truest and toughest feelings. Not surprisingly, this often evolves into an unhelpful form of self-talk. We whisper messages like this to ourselves: "God doesn't want to hear my complaints or troubles. It's best to stuff them all deep and keep them to myself."

But what if I told you the truth was just the opposite? Would it surprise you if I told you that more than one Scripture verse invites our total honesty, transparency, and—yes—even our complaints?

First Peter 5:7 urges you to "cast all your anxiety on Him because He cares about you." In Christ's parable of the persistent widow, He asks pointedly, "Will God not bring about justice for His elect who cry out to Him day and night, and will He delay long for them?" (Luke 18:7).

Would you believe that God loves you so much that He even loves to hear your complaints and troubles? That's David's testimony. He offers us the kind of self-talk we need to think rightly about things that feel wrong.

Listen to this commentary of his prayer life in Psalm 142:2. David says, "I pour out my complaint before Him; I declare my trouble before Him."

Were you expecting that? It's quite a departure from the pastoral prayer of Psalm 23 or David's declaration in Psalm 34:1, "I will bless the Lord at all times; His praise shall continually be in my mouth."

Though David is frank about his sin and need for forgiveness in Psalms 32 and 51 ("wash me, and I will be whiter than snow" NIV), admitting our disappointments with God—and to God—is altogether different.

But can we really pour out our complaints before God? Can we really declare our trouble before Him? Yes—and yes, Elsewhere in Psalm 62:8, David implores us, "Pour out your hearts before Him; God is a refuge for us." That's quite an invitation. It's entirely different than how many of us pray.

On this issue of transparency with God, Dr. Ed Welch argues,

> If there is anything we know about ourselves and Scripture, we know this: we were made to speak both the joys and sorrows of our heart to the Lord. He delights in hearing our joys and shouldering our sorrows. The most human thing we can do is call out to him. Any system that restrains the cry of the heart is suspect at best. More than likely, it has diabolic fingerprints on it.[1]

HOW TO MAKE THIS SELF-TALK YOURS

It all sounds remarkably freeing. But how do we internalize this? What do we need to do to make David's self-talk *our* self-talk? Honestly, I think David hands us the two keys inside this verse.

1. Pour Out Your Complaint Before God

Be specific, respectful, and completely honest. There's no point in trying to hide your complaint. If you've thought it, God knows it. As David reminds us in Psalm 139:4, "Even before there is a word on my tongue, behold, LORD, you know it all." You won't surprise God, but in my own experience, you'll be pleasantly surprised with how good it feels just to let Him know how you feel.

2. Declare Your Troubles Before God

Go ahead and list them all. Hold nothing back. The Hebrew word for *trouble* that David uses can include adversary, adversity, affliction, anguish, distress, tribulation, or problem of any kind. What's on your list? Give it to God. All of it. By the way, I find it helpful to do this aloud. Audibly expressing your thoughts drives home the fact that this is a real conversation with the real living God.

Notice, though, that we are instructed to pour out our complaints "before Him." We are to declare our troubles "before Him." The alternative is to bring our complaints to *others*, which only serves to discourage their spirits. Charles Spurgeon cautions, "We may complain to God, but not of God. When we complain, it should not be before men, but before God alone."[2]

Let that standard be yours—and mine.

• • •

SAY IT

"I pour out my complaint before Him; I declare my trouble before Him."

PSALM 142:2

PRAY IT

O Lord—

I don't want to be known as a whiner. Not on Earth—and more importantly, not in heaven.

But Lord, You know the adversity I face. You know every anguish, every nagging anxiety.

Let this be the first of many frank conversations between us.

Hear me now as I pour out my complaint about:

________________________.

Lord, here's what else is on my list of troubles: __________.

I've come to You with these things because I don't know what to do about them.

But You do. You're the only One with the answers.

O Lord, hear me, please. Show me what to do. I simply do not know!

But thank You that I know You. Be my Waymaker, I humbly ask.

Lord, I believe. Please help me in my unbelief.

Amen.

“ 39 ”

REMEMBER TO REMEMBER

I remember the days of old;
I meditate on all Your accomplishments;
I reflect on the work of Your hands.

PSALM 143:5

You could almost set your watch with it. Typically, an hour after supper, our boy, Timmy, would ask, “Hey, when are we going to eat supper?”

“We already did,” I would counter.

“No, we didn’t.”

“Yes, we did.”

“Well, what did we have?” Timmy would parry, certain he was going to win the match.

“We had spaghetti, remember? It was *you* who asked Mom to make it. And she even baked the brownies you love!”

“Oh, yeah,” he would finally concede, adding, “Well, I’m still hungry.”

To say he forgot his mother’s work of planning, cooking, and cleaning up that meal was an understatement, but at age five, we had to give him some slack. What about grown-ups like you and me? How careful are *we* to recall God's work in our lives? Is it possible we have "memory issues"?

Personally, I have four problems in life: counting, remembering, and counting. Maybe you can relate? One realist defined memory as—the thing one forgets with. Sadly, most of us have a better "forgetter" than a "rememberer." On the other hand, there are a lot of people who never forget a kind deed—if they did it!

Back to my original question. Do you struggle with remembering God's goodness to you? I do. Rich in gifts, we are poor in thanks. Dressed in Gucci, we praise like paupers. Spiritually speaking, God has blessed every believer with a Rolex lifestyle, but we don't seem to have the time to remember all He has done in and through us.

Our selective memory (let's call it what it is) often stems from a self-indulgence in poor self-talk. We say, "My life is so busy that I multitask even when sleeping! God knows I'm grateful, so there's no need to obsess over rehearsing the good things He's done for me. I have too much on my mind to reflect on it all. I'm pretty sure God's okay with that."

Except He isn't.

Remembering God's works and goodness in your life is a biblical command, not an optional accessory. Here's a quick review of just a few of the verses with the word "remember" italicized for our attention.

"You are to *remember* the Lord your God, for it is He who is giving you power to make wealth, in order to confirm His covenant which He swore to your fathers, as it is this day" (Deuteronomy 8:18).

"*Remember* also your Creator in the days of your youth, before the evil days come and the years approach when you will say, 'I have no pleasure in them'" (Ecclesiastes 12:1).

"When I saw their fear, I stood and said to the nobles, the officials, and the rest of the people: 'Do not be afraid of them; *remember* the Lord who is great and awesome, and fight for your brothers, your sons, your daughters, your wives, and your houses'" (Nehemiah 4:14).

Remembering is such a big deal to Christ that at the very heart of the communion service we celebrate at church, He has commanded us to remember what He has done:

> When He had given thanks, He broke it and said, "This is My body, which is for you; do this in *remembrance* of Me." In the same way He also took the cup after supper, saying, "This cup is the new covenant in My blood; do this, as often as you drink it, in *remembrance* of Me" (1 Corinthians 11:24-25).

You say, "Okay, I get it. But I need some help here. This praise stuff doesn't come naturally to me." Good news! The shepherd-king David has better self-talk for us than the wimpy excuses many of us use. In Psalm 143:5, he lets us in on his strategy. Keep in mind that David penned this thought when he was hunkered down in a cave, hiding from Saul, who was determined to run a sword right through David's belly. At that moment life was not good, but David knew that *God* was. And in the middle of his darkness, David shares this light with you and me: "I remember the days of old; I meditate on all Your accomplishments; I reflect on the work of Your hands" (Psalm 143:5).

HOW TO MAKE THIS SELF-TALK YOURS

I'm neither a theologian nor a genius—and I'm guessing you aren't either. But it sure seems like David is handing us a three-point strategy we can copy immediately.

Strategy #1: I Remember

A disproportionately large chunk of this remembering business has to do with choice. When it comes to God's goodness, much will be forgotten unless we choose to remember it. Our problem is not the inability to remember so much as our unwillingness to try.

Anglican Samuel Johnson asserted, "The true art of memory is the art of attention."[1]

Attention is something you choose to give—or not give. It's time we gave attention to what God has done in our lives and on our behalf. It's time to remember.

Strategy #2: I Meditate

To meditate is to ponder slowly at a deeper level. Think of the unhurried way a cow chews and chews (and chews) its cud. They're in no hurry. They are savoring every morsel to the max. We can do the same thing spiritually (minus the moos) when we carve out regular times to pause and ponder God's work in us. A word of caution: Our culture has not schooled us in this *at all.* Unlike cows, we approach the web and the larger world, inhaling information without digesting it, let alone chewing on it. Meditating on God's goodness is a discipline that will take time.

Strategy #3: I Reflect

The third action step here is to reflect. But how is that different from remembering or meditating? I looked up the word *reflect* and was intrigued by *Merriam-Webster*'s explanation. It means to make apparent, express, or manifest; to cause (something, like honor or credit) to be attributed or associated.[2]

What we're really talking about here is making God's story in your life famous to everyone in your circle. And don't overlook those two words "honor" and "credit." That's what God is looking for.

One blizzardy morning, I was driving on the expressway into Chicago when I hit a patch of black ice. Our minivan spun around, the front end striking a cement divider, ultimately stopping at 90 degrees to the flow of rush hour traffic. (A polite way of saying the car's rear end was really in the way!) In God's kindness, no one else hit the minivan, a friend came to pick me up, and insurance covered the repair.

Every single time since then, when I'm driving into the city and come to that spot on the expressway, I remember, and I lift my heart in thanksgiving to God. And I reflect.

What's your story? God longs to hear it!

• • •

“SAY IT”

“I remember the days of old; I meditate on all Your accomplishments; I reflect on the work of Your hands.”

PSALM 143:5

“PRAY IT”

Heavenly Father—

Thank You for the countless ways You have protected, delivered, and provided for me.

Forgive me for the ingratitude of my silence.

I wish to learn this lifestyle of remembering Your goodness.

Please show me. Teach me. I am a slow learner.

But I am a learner who loves You, Lord.

I pray this in the name of Jesus, with unending thanks for Your unending goodness.

Amen.

PRAISE HIM WHILE YOU CAN

I will praise the Lord *while I live;*
I will sing praises to my God while I have my being.

PSALM 146:2

It was a strange way to spend a Saturday morning—planning a funeral for my mom.

Walking past her writing desk, I found her spiral-bound appointment calendar, filled with birthdays and anniversary notes, all penned in her schoolteacher's handwriting. Few people were as faithful at sending cards or remembering whatever special event you were celebrating. But she would neither sign nor send a single card again. Those opportunities were gone when death came.

This being the final chapter in the book, it's fitting to think about final things. My purpose is not to depress you but to energize you. Specifically, I want you (and me) to be more intentional about praising God while we can.

Just before Memorial Day weekend, so many customers lined up at the fuel pumps that the corner gas station became a traffic jam. The place oozed with impatient customers, like the pastor who stood in line "for an eternity," he said, to fill up. Upon paying the attendant, the cashier apologized, saying, "Seems like everybody waits until the last minute to get ready for a long trip." The pastor smiled wryly and said, "I know what you mean. I have the same problem in my line of work."

Oddly, our tendency to procrastinate is no more evident than in the way that we praise—or don't praise. Nothing feels more optional, more "pretty-good-idea-ish" than developing the discipline to praise God gushingly. Like changing a furnace filter, we know it's something we should do. Someday.

That sleepy-sloppy attitude degenerates into a negative self-talk we would be horrified to own publicly. But it's there. In our minds, we say things such as, "I'll get around to praising God when I have a little more time. Right now, I'm just trying to survive 'real life.'" Right.

Not many saw as much real life as David did. You've seen example after example in this book. But at some point, he learned that praise is never optional and, in fact, it's always intentional. We somehow get the idea that praising just comes naturally to some folks more than others, so we're off the hook if we're not one of those "praise people."

Biblically speaking, God has uniquely gifted some of us to teach, but that doesn't excuse any parent from failing to teach their kids. God wired some of us to be evangelists, but that doesn't excuse the rest of us from sharing our faith. While it's true some personality types might well lean toward a praise mindset, guess what? We're all called to praise.

Listen to David's self-talk in Psalm 146:2. He declares, "I will praise the Lord while I live; I will sing praises to my God while I have my being." I love the nuances of the multifaceted Hebrew word for "praise" used here, *hala*. Biblical praise means to boast, shine, celebrate, and rave.

Imagine God's pleasure when we say, "Only the Lord could have worked that out. He is so amazing!" But if His pleasure is on your mind, you can also shine a spotlight on God with a job well done, a house well cleaned, and a song well sung. Even a child can celebrate God with a painting or drawing. Praise is much more than a song or speech.

What would it look like for you to boast about God? To rave about Him? That's what David has in mind for us. That's the lifestyle we're called to learn. It turns out the self-talk in Psalm 146:2, like all the best self-talk, is not about self at all. It's entirely about God and His goodness and greatness.

You say, "I'm okay with praising when life is good. But what about when life stinks?" Just a quick reminder that in a span of just a few hours, Job lost all his sons, daughters, servants, oxen, sheep, camels, donkeys—not to mention his health. But his response was still one of praise. In Job 1:21, he testified, "The LORD gave and the LORD has taken away. Blessed be the name of the LORD."

Praise in the face of loss or hurt makes no sense on a human level. But you and I aren't praising a human. God is always worthy, even when our feelings say otherwise. And—here's the crazy thing—the act of choosing to praise God when we don't feel like it comes back to bless us. In the inexplicable calculus of God, He blesses us even as we bless Him. I can't explain the math, but I know it's true.

Recently, I powered up my computer, and it would not recognize my hard drive. Imagine the loss of all that data—photos, video clips, and a thousand other things I should have backed up but didn't. There were unfinished sermons, blogs, and book chapters—all about to be lost.

Typically, my initial reaction to setbacks like this is to hyperventilate while curling up into an emotional ball of acid-laden anxiety. Not this time. This time, I deliberately chose to praise God. I got down on my knees, lifted my hands to heaven, and prayed, "Lord, I give You praise anyway. This situation is a mess, but I choose to praise You now, even before there's an answer. Even if an answer never comes." The sense of calm, peace, and reassurance that came over me was remarkable—to the point of supernatural. The calculus of God! (And yes, against all odds, that computer finally came back to life to the glory and praise of God.)

HOW TO MAKE THIS SELF-TALK YOURS

That takes us to the pivotal phrases "while I live" and "while I have my being." David prioritizes the end in view. He knows there will come a time when he will have run out of time. No longer will he be able to praise. Best seize the moment. And the next. And the next. Until there are no more.

Turns out, there's a fixed number of sunrises and sunsets you'll see. A limited number of Christmases you'll celebrate. And babies you'll cuddle. Praise is possible now, even in this broken world. But it's a limited-time deal.

I once heard a preacher talk about his hospitalized friend battling an excruciating form of cancer. The preacher remarked that whenever he visited this friend, the guy was upbeat and full of godly encouragement and praise. None of this was lost on the doctors and nurses attending him. One day, the preacher asked the guy point blank, "How do you do it? You admit that some days are agonizing, and you know this cancer is going to kill you. How do you maintain your outlook?" Quietly and confidently came the reply, "What you say is all true. I know how this ends. But think! These days—these moments—are my very last opportunities to praise God in the presence of His enemies."

That guy was prioritizing with the end in view. He finished well. And now it's our turn.

• • •

SAY IT

"I will praise the L*ORD while I live; I will sing praises to my God while I have my being."*

PSALM 146:2

PRAY IT

Lord,

My time is fleeting.

Life on Earth is a temporary loan, and it is Your right to expect a return on that loan.

Let my praise show compound interest.

Help me learn the art, discipline, and delight of praising You.

Even when there are no answers.

Even when there seems to be no hope.

Let me stand in line with Job, Daniel, Habakkuk, and all those throughout the ages who chose to make their lives more about their praise than their problems.

Amen.

AFTERWORD

Now what?

It's great that you made it through this book, but that doesn't automatically make you a conquering hero in the battle for your mind. Take it from me, someone with a long history of "stinkin' thinkin." No one can fix their self-talk overnight, but anyone can take a step in the right direction. Better than that, anyone can and will benefit immediately from the tiniest effort at biblical self-talk.

I wrote this book because I've seen what biblical self-talk can do. That doesn't mean I've progressed to spiritual grandeur and unbroken success. I'm still broken—a learner whose primary qualification for writing this book is a lifetime of poor self-talk. I know what these battles are like.

But my appetite has been stoked by what I've seen God do. I'm hungry for more. Much more. And I'm also eager for you to taste that banquet of better thinking.

Now that we've reached the end, where should you begin? Clearly, you can't work on all of these verses simultaneously. But you had better work on one or two. Or three. Otherwise, reading this book offers you nothing more than a few hours of distraction.

Which should you choose? That's easy, but it's also very personal. Do a quick inventory and try to assess the following:

- What is the most ferocious fear haunting your free moments of thought?
- What unwelcome "thought guest" roams the hallways of your mind night after night like a squatter demanding permanent residency?
- What is beating you up again and again—the sin you're weary of confessing over and over?

Find a verse in this book that addresses your concern and run with it! Here's a practical strategy that will equip you to do that.

MEMORIZE THE VERSES YOU NEED MOST

The act of memorizing these Scriptures reclaims brain space currently occupied by negative thought patterns. It's not enough to chase away the bad guys, though. We have to replace unhelpful, unbiblical notions with godly convictions. Take back what is good and godly by replacing the negative garbage with biblical truth you've committed to memory.

FORM BETTER BIBLICAL SELF-TALK

Quoting these verses (out loud) begins to reshape and reform your self-talk. There is no better self-talk than pure Scripture. We must speak God's truth to every lie that sneaks (or is directly deposited by our enemy) into our minds. And never underestimate the deadly hiss of your adversary, who delights in whispering anything and everything untrue. Commit to speaking the truth the very instant the lies come at you. You'll notice that every chapter in this book ends with the two-pronged strategy of "Say It" and "Pray It." That's more than a cute slogan. Let it be a way of life for you.

CELEBRATE EVERY WIN

You have beaten up yourself enough. It's time to celebrate. This is critical because every time you celebrate a small victory in your struggle, you are exposing the lie that says you can't win. Celebrating smaller victories sets you up for more significant victories. Romans 15:13 strongly says, "May the God of hope fill you with all joy and peace in believing, so that you will abound in hope by the power of the Holy Spirit." Hope feels good every time. And celebrating small victories ushers in bigger victories.

Celebrating small victories points to the superiority of Jesus in you. As 1 John 4:4 reminds us, "Greater is He who is in you." Any victory you ever experience in life is a Jesus thing. So shouldn't He get the credit? When we point to the superiority of Jesus in us, it has the wonderfully soothing effect of taking the burden off our shoulders. If Jesus is superior, and Jesus gives the victory, then shouldn't this be all about *Jesus* and very little about me and my concerns—or you and your concerns?

KEEP COMING BACK

Your negative self-talk didn't start overnight, and developing biblical self-talk will likely not be instantaneous. It sure hasn't been for me. But progress is possible starting today.

I'm reminded of the summer when Diana and I decided to replace a large patch of hostas in our yard with new grass. Though I dug up the hostas in early spring, some survivors emerged, poking through the dirt. I dug them up too, and I was convinced I'd won the battle. But in just days, still more hostas were popping up. These, too, were rooted out, after which I planted the grass seed.

Please don't laugh when I tell you that I cheered for every green blade that eked through the dirt, only to groan at the emergence of still more hostas—which I faithfully plucked. This cycle went on for weeks. And then months. And then you know what happened? Eventually, enough grass—the stuff we wanted—took root and crowded out the last of the hostas—the stuff we didn't want.

I think you get the point. It's going to take work. It's going to take time. But God has willed you to win. You have the seeds. Now, get out there and plant!

NOTES

CHAPTER 1: SLEEP SAFE, LIVE SAFE

1. "What Are Sleep Deprivation and Deficiency?," National Heart, Lung, and Blood Institute, updated March 24, 2022, https://www.nhlbi.nih.gov/health-topics/sleep-deprivation-and-deficiency.
2. Marco Hafner, Martin Stepanek, et al., "Why Sleep Matters—The Economic Costs of Insufficient Sleep: A Cross-Country Comparative Analysis," PubMed, January 1, 2017, https://pubmed.ncbi.nlm.nih.gov/28983434/.
3. Eric Suni, "100+ Sleep Statistics," Sleep Foundation, updated September 26, 2023, https://www.sleepfoundation.org/how-sleep-works/sleep-facts-statistics#our-sleep-cycles.
4. Cynthia Reuben, "QuickStats: Percentage of Adults Aged > 18 Years Who Took Medication To Help Fall or Stay Asleep Four or More Times in the Past Week, by Sex and Age Group—National Health Interview Survey, United States, 2017–2018," CDC, December 13, 2019, https://www.cdc.gov/mmwr/volumes/68/wr/mm6849a5.htm?s_cid=mm6849a5_w.
5. "The Issue of Knock-offs in Fashion," Indiana University Bloomington Libraries, updated February 10, 2025, https://guides.libraries.indiana.edu/fashion-ethics/knockoffs.

CHAPTER 2: AT YOUR RIGHT HAND

1. Tim Tebow, *Shaken: Discovering Your True Identity in the Midst of Life's Storms* (Colorado Springs: Waterbrook, 2016), 79.

CHAPTER 3: HEART'S INTENT

1. Amy Tikkanen, "Tsar Bomba," Britannica, https://www.britannica.com/topic/Tsar-Bomba.

CHAPTER 4: BECAUSE HE DELIGHTED IN ME

1. Jeff Tavss, "Heroic students who saved mother, children are rewarded with Jazz tickets," Fox 13, December 11, 2023, https://www.fox13now.com/news/local-news/heroic-students-who-saved-mother-children-rewarded-with-jazz-tickets.
2. Charles H. Spurgeon, "The Treasury of David: Psalm 18," The Spurgeon Archive, https://archive.spurgeon.org/treasury/ps018.php.

CHAPTER 5: WHEN YOU'RE ON GOD'S SIDE

1. Barnes' Notes on the Whole Bible, "Bible Commentaries, Psalms 18," StudyLight, https://www.studylight.org/commentaries/eng/bnb/psalms-18.html.

CHAPTER 6: BOASTING—WRONG WAY, RIGHT WAY

1. Stefanie Dazio, Brian Melley, and David Koenig, "US officials: Pilot error caused Kobe Bryant chopper crash," AP News, February 9, 2021, https://apnews.com/article/kobe-bryant-helicopter-crash-cause-2c87b04d28961fd277927eea8e8e5564.
2. Stefanie Dazio, Brian Melley, and David Koenig, "US officials: Pilot error caused Kobe Bryant chopper crash," AP News, February 9, 2021, https://apnews.com/article/kobe-bryant-helicopter-crash-cause-2c87b04d28961fd277927eea8e8e5564.

CHAPTER 7: FREEDOM FROM NETS

1. Jordan T. Prodanoff, "How Many Ads Do We See a Day? 17 Insightful Stats," Web tribunal, updated March 6, 2023, https://webtribunal.net/blog/how-many-ads-do-we-see-a-day/#gref.

CHAPTER 8: ON LEVEL GROUND

1. "What is the flattest state in the United States? And the most mountainous?," WGN9, August 1, 2017, https://wgntv.com/weather/what-is-the-flattest-state-in-the-united-states-and-the-most-mountainous/.
2. Cory Price, "The 10 Flattest Countries In The World," WorldAtlas, November 29, 2022, https://www.worldatlas.com/geography/10-flattest-countries-in-the-world.html.
3. Stephen M. Smith, "Understanding the Dangers of Slips, Trips, and Falls," Smith Law Center, July 1, 2024, https://www.smithlawcenter.com/blog/statistics-slips-trips-and-falls#:~:text=Poor%20lighting%2C%20cluttered%20walkways%2C%20and,to%2055%25%20of%20these%20incidents.

CHAPTER 9: BIG GOD, SMALL BULLY

1. Katherine Schaeffer, "9 facts about bullying in the U.S.," Pew Research Center, November 17, 2023, https://www.pewresearch.org/short-reads/2023/11/17/9-facts-about-bullying-in-the-us/.
2. "Facts About Bullying," stopbullying.gov, https://www.stopbullying.gov/media/facts/index.html.
3. James Jackson, "The average NFL player height and weight by position," Critical Body, updated June 24, 2023, https://criticalbody.com/average-nfl-height/.

CHAPTER 10: HIDE-AND-SEEK

1. St. Augustine of Hippo, *Confessions* (New York: Barnes and Noble, 1992), 21.
2. Erin Leyba, "10 Proven Ways to Make a Baby Feel Loved," Psychology Today, updated February 17, 2024, https://www.psychologytoday.com/us/blog/joyful-parenting/202401/10-science-backed-ways-to-help-babies-feel-loved.
3. Charles H. Spurgeon, "The Treasury of David: Psalm 27," The Spurgeon Archive, https://archive.spurgeon.org/treasury/ps027.php.

CHAPTER 11: DON'T HATE TO WAIT

1. Michelle Willard, "Survey says 'patience no longer reality,'" Daily News Journal, February 23, 2015, https://www.dnj.com/story/money/business/2015/02/23/survey-says-patience-longer-reality/23903981/#.
2. Judy Nelson, "Waiting on God," The Banner, January 18, 2011, https://www.thebanner.org/features/2011/01/waiting-on-god.

CHAPTER 12: CONSTANT PRAISE

1. Matthew Henry, "Psalm 150," Blue Letter Bible, https://www.blueletterbible.org/comm/mhc/psa/psa_150.cfm.

CHAPTER 13: BRAG ON GOD, ENCOURAGE OTHERS

1. William Law, *A Serious Call to a Devout and Holy Life* (Grand Rapids, MI: Christian Classics Ethereal Library), PDF download, https://www.ntslibrary.com/PDF%20Books/Law%20A%20Serious%20Call%20to%20a%20Devout%20and%20Holy%20Life.pdf.
2. Calvin's Commentaries, "Psalm 35," Bible Hub, https://biblehub.com/commentaries/calvin/psalms/35.htm.
3. John Calvin, "Psalm 34," Christian Classics Ethereal Library, https://www.ccel.org/study/Psalm_34:3.

CHAPTER 14: SEEK GOD, FIND ANSWERS

1. "10 MOST COMMON PHOBIAS & FEARS," Baptist Health, September 22, 2020, https://www.baptisthealth.com/blog/family-health/10-most-common-phobias-fears.
2. Theo Tsaousides, "Why Are We Scared of Public Speaking?," Psychology Today, November 27, 2017, https://www.psychologytoday.com/us/blog/smashing-the-brainblocks/201711/why-are-we-scared-of-public-speaking.

CHAPTER 15: DEPART FROM EVIL

1. Ryan Carrigan, "Moving Industry Statistics," moveBuddha, updated February 7, 2025, https://www.movebuddha.com/blog/moving-industry-statistics/.

CHAPTER 17: WHEN BROKEN AND CRUSHED

1. "Is Broken Heart Syndrome Real?," American Heart Association, last reviewed May 31, 2024, https://www.heart.org/en/health-topics/cardiomyopathy/what-is-cardiomyopathy-in-adults/is-broken-heart-syndrome-real.
2. Charles H. Spurgeon, "Treasury of David: Psalm 34," Grace Gems, https://gracegems.org/Spurgeon/034.htm.
3. Oswald Chambers, *My Utmost for His Highest*, (Uhrichsville, OH: Barbour Publishing, Inc., 1987), 240.

CHAPTER 18: THOROUGHLY DELIGHTED!

1. "Grandma Got Run Over by a Reindeer" was written in 1977 © by Randy Brooks.

2. "How Many Orders Does Amazon Get & Deliver Per Day?," Capital One Shopping, updated April 15, 2025, https://capitaloneshopping.com/research/amazon-orders-per-day/#:~:text=On%20an%20average%20day%2C%20Amazon,or%208%2C298%20orders%20per%20minute.

3. Charles Wesley, "The Journal of Charles Wesley, September 1–November 6, 1739," Sermon Index, https://www.sermonindex.net/modules/articles/index.php?view=article&aid=26140.

4. Charles H. Spurgeon, "The Treasury of David: Psalm 37," The Spurgeon Archive, https://archive.spurgeon.org/treasury/ps037.php.

5. Max Lucado, "The Longings of Your Heart," Max Lucado, https://maxlucado.com/listen/the-longings-of-your-heart/.

CHAPTER 20: DON'T FEED THE FEARS!

1. DeeDee Correll, "Colorado woman who fed bears is killed by one," Los Angeles Times, August 12, 2009, https://www.latimes.com/archives/la-xpm-2009-aug-12-na-bear-attack12-story.html.

CHAPTER 21: MOPE OR HOPE

1. "2025 Compare Climate & Weather: Chicago, IL vs Duluth, MN," https://www.bestplaces.net/climate/?c1=51714000&c2=52717000.

2. Sian Ferguson, "Top 10 Life-Stressors That Can Trigger Anxiety," PsychCentral, updated July 27, 2022, https://psychcentral.com/stress/top-10-life-stressors-that-can-trigger-anxiety#top-10-life-stressors.

3. *What About Bob?*, directed by Frank Oz (Burbank, CA: Touchstone Pictures, 1991).

CHAPTER 24: A HOME FOR THE EMOTIONALLY HOMELESS

1. Brian Glassman, "New Survey Data Provides Demographic Profile of Population Experiencing Homelessness Who Lived in Emergency and Transitional Shelters," United States Census Bureau, February 27, 2024, https://www.census.gov/library/stories/2024/02/living-in-shelters.html.

2. Dennis Thompson, "Loneliness Is Plaguing Americans in 2024: Poll," US News, February 1, 2024, https://www.usnews.com/news/health-news/articles/2024-02-01/loneliness-is-plaguing-americans-in-2024-poll.

3. Nicole K. Valtora, Mona Kanaan, et al., "Loneliness and social isolation as risk factors for coronary heart disease and stroke: systematic review and meta-analysis of longitudinal observational studies," National Library of Medicine, April 18, 2016, https://pubmed.ncbi.nlm.nih.gov/27091846/.

4. Mother Teresa, *A Simple Path* (New York: Ballantine Books, 1995), 79.

CHAPTER 26: ESCAPE FROM DEATH—YOURS!

1. "Leading Causes of Death," Centers for Disease Control and Prevention, June 5, 2025, https://www.cdc.gov/nchs/fastats/leading-causes-of-death.htm.

2. "NSC Estimates Traffic Crashes Took More Than 44,000 Lives in 2023," NSC, February 26, 2024, https://www.nsc.org/newsroom/nsc-estimates-traffic-crashes-took-more-than-44,00.

3. Shelby Simon, "How Many People Die From Car Accidents Each Year?," Forbes, updated October 10, 2022, https://www.forbes.com/advisor/legal/auto-accident/car-accident-deaths/.

4. The Treasury of David, "Psalm 68:20," Bible Hub, https://biblehub.com/commentaries/psalms/68-20.htm.

5. The Treasury of David, "Psalm 68:20," Bible Hub, https://biblehub.com/commentaries/psalms/68-20.htm.

CHAPTER 27: SAY IT AGAIN. AND AGAIN!

1. Constance Craig Smith, "Growing up Getty: Biography details billionaire's extravagant life—including charging interest on a loan to save his grandson's life," Daily Mail, updated August 18, 2022, https://www.dailymail.co.uk/home/article-11124903/Growing-Getty-Biography-details-billionaires-extravagant-life.html.

2. Matthew Henry, "Psalm 70," Blue Letter Bible, https://www.blueletterbible.org/comm/mhc/psa/psa_070.cfm.

CHAPTER 29: KNEEL FIRST. KNEEL ALWAYS.

1. Jamie Ballard, "Most American men own at least one suit, but 28% never wear one," YouGov, June 18, 2024, https://today.yougov.com/society/articles/49799-most-american-men-own-a-suit-28-percent-never-wear-one-poll.

CHAPTER 30: I MUST LEARN TO HATE

1. Charles H. Spurgeon, "The Treasury of David: Psalm 101," The Spurgeon Archive, https://archive.spurgeon.org/treasury/ps101.php.

2. Charles H. Spurgeon, "The Treasury of David: Psalm 101," The Spurgeon Archive, https://archive.spurgeon.org/treasury/ps101.php.

CHAPTER 33: YOUR SINS ARE GONE—TOTALLY GONE

1. Charles H. Spurgeon, "The Treasury of David: Psalm 103," The Spurgeon Archive, https://archive.spurgeon.org/treasury/ps103.php.

CHAPTER 38: GIVE HIM YOUR COMPLAINTS

1. *No More Minimizing Pain*, blog by Ed Welch, The Christian Counseling & Educational Foundation, April 14, 2016, https://www.ccef.org/no-more-minimizing-pain.

2. Charles H. Spurgeon, "The Treasury of David: Psalm 142," The Spurgeon Archive, https://archive.spurgeon.org/treasury/ps142.php.

CHAPTER 39: REMEMBER TO REMEMBER

1. Samuel Johnson, "No. 74. Memory rarely deficient," Samuel Johnson's Essays, September 15, 1759, https://www.johnsonessays.com/the-idler/memory-rarely-deficient/.

2. "Reflect," Merriam-Webster, updated June 10, 2025, https://www.merriam-webster.com/dictionary/reflect.

BIBLE COPYRIGHT NOTIFICATIONS

To learn more about Harvest House books and to read sample chapters, visit our website:

www.HarvestHousePublishers.com